BE

30 PROVEN TOOLS FOR HEALING FROM SEXUAL BROKENNESS

RICHARD THOMPSON
FOREWORD BY: JOHN DAWSON

BE FREE
30 Proven Tools to Find Freedom from Sexual Brokenness

© Richard Thompson 2025

All rights reserved. No part of this book may be reproduced, stored in a retrieval system, or transmitted in any form or by any means, electronic, mechanical, photocopying, recording or otherwise, without the prior permission of the author.

Unless otherwise stated, Scripture quotations are from the ESV® Bible (The Holy Bible, English Standard Version®), © 2001 by Crossway, a publishing ministry of Good News Publishers. Used by permission. All rights reserved.

ISBN 979-8-342496-82-7
Printed in the United States

For questions or to reach the author:
Befree4ever777@gmail.com

What Others Are Saying

"This book has been a game-changer for me. It exposed the root issues behind my struggles but also provided practical steps to overcome them. The insights and tools shared in it have given me hope and confidence to walk in freedom. I've seen real change in my life, and it's given me the strength to confront and overcome challenges I once thought were impossible. The way this book speaks directly to the heart while offering clear, actionable steps is truly powerful. I'm incredibly grateful for this resource, and I believe it will make a lasting impact on anyone who reads it."

...

"Reading this book has given me a pathway to hope in a life that has only known hopelessness and confusion in my addiction. Its practical steps make it goal-orientated, which helps me and my personality type improve and grow more than mere self-awareness could ever do. These steps have given me more understanding of my hurt and brokenness (present and past), but it hasn't left me there; it's given me a sense of safety and clarity regarding my issues, and vision for a life of freedom!"

...

"The tools in this book were absolutely pivotal in transforming my life. Each one I applied strengthened me to live a life of purity and freedom in God. Seek God, apply these tools, and BE FREE!"

"I have been using tools from Richard's book, as well as just learning from his life, community and communion with the Holy Spirit, for the last year and a half. As a result, I have experienced more transformation in the area of purity and surrender to Jesus than I ever have in my entire life. Rich is a man full of wisdom who honors and abides in the Holy Spirit. His desire is that men and women would be set free to be all that Jesus created them to be. In a time when a high percentage of the world struggles with sexual immorality, including pastors and leaders, now is the time that we need to take this conversation seriously on a global scale. May we be a people who worship our Lord with pure hearts and true intentions."

...

"Reading this book helped me realize that I am not alone. I saw that other guys could relate to my sexual addiction, and that many started where I was. The toolkit helped me to identify the triggers and what drove me to act out."

...

"The toolkit is super-practical and meets me where I am. I am so thankful for the victories I have seen in my life as a result."

...

"This book has been a game-changer for me. For the first time, I discovered a practical tool that not only helps me and my friends avoid acting out, but also shows us how to rewire our minds. Most resources deal with the aftermath of sexual addiction, but this book empowers you to take action even before the big temptation comes and change the patterns that lead to harmful behaviors. It offers a clear, actionable plan for breaking free from addiction and moving beyond just hoping for a good month. Truly revolutionary!"

...

"This book is something I wish I'd had many years ago. These tools are needed to combat sexual sin at any and every stage. This is a book that has helped me have hope for breakthrough and equipped me to stand up and fight. Apply it with courage, and I believe you will see the change in your life and the ones you walk with just like I have! I am so thankful for this book, and I believe you will be too!"

...

"The tools in this book have given me the capability to see clearly. For too long, we addicts stumbled in blind pain and brokenness, not knowing where we were stepping. These tools have allowed me to see the big, complicated knot that my addiction is so that I can begin pulling on strands by the guidance of God. It's like opening the blinds in a dark room: you can finally see what a mess it is, and you can finally start cleaning things up."

Dedication

For the One who brings freedom,
And to those who are wanting to receive it

Acknowledgments

I want to thank the following people:

Mark and John-Mark Dyer, a formidable father-and-son team who encouraged me to develop this book, even though I didn't want to write it. Thanks also to John-Mark for editing my original (even shorter!) edition.

Andy Butcher, my editor—for the exhilarating and challenging experience this has been.

My original sponsor in Sex Addicts Anonymous—you know who you are. You taught me so many of the tools and truths that are in this book. May the Lord reward you for what you have shared with me in anonymity.

My two counselors across the three-and-a-half years of my initial recovery: Steve Thomas and dear Pat Caven, who suddenly passed away last year and was like an older sister to me for more than 30 years. Again, words cannot express how much I owe you two for the wisdom and tools that are in this book. It's always amazing to me that the Lord can hide such giants among us so well. (Hint: They are there if you seek them out.)

My four kids, who still love me and forgive me, despite what I did to them through my brokenness.

My second family and tribe of Youth With A Mission, which I became a part of in 1986 and where I remain to this day. Thank you for your servant leadership and love and for giving me a "home."

And finally, to you the reader—may you truly find the freedom that you need.

Contents

What Others Are Saying — 3
Dedication — 6
Acknowledgments — 7
Foreword — 9
Introduction — 11

SECTION ONE
The Small Hammer: Habit/Early Compulsion — 18

SECTION TWO
The Medium-sized Hammer: Middle-to
Late-Compulsion to Early Addiction — 39

SECTION THREE
The Sledgehammer: Late Compulsion
to Addiction — 65

Afterword — 93
Understanding the Cycle of Addiction — 97
Assessing Your Situation — 100
About the Author — 103

Foreword

I'm very grateful for this book. Thank you, Richard. This is one man's story honestly told. It is also a gift from the heavenly Father to you and me. I know it advertises thirty steps, and yes, it is immensely practical; however, this story most importantly reveals who God is.

You will experience new levels of healing and comfort, new levels of revelation of the love and mercy of God. Jesus reveals the longsuffering Father who is the friend of sinners, the only One who can deliver His children from prisons of shame, compulsion and deception.

The Psalmist spoke of the one who ... "forgives all our sins and heals all our diseases, who redeems our life from the pit and crowns you with love and compassion, who satisfies your desires with good things so that your youth is renewed like the eagles." Ps. 103:2-5.

Are you weary and discouraged? Are you a little reluctant to approach a part of your life that is overshadowed with pain and repeated failure? It is no coincidence that you hold this book in your hand. You are a creation of God. You are a person of unique quality, beauty and value. You are loved. Richard's story is an invitation to a new day. A conversation begins now as you find a quiet place and turn these pages. You are entering a relationship with the most tender, loving personality one could ever know. God has fathered Richard and God will father you. "As a Father has compassion on His children, so the Lord has compassion on those who fear Him; for He knows how we are formed, He remembers that we are dust." Ps. 103:13-14.

Because our Creator "knows how we are formed" He also knows the next simple steps on our personal pathways to wholeness and joy. That's right, simple steps. Richard has provided a thoughtful, insightful guide that is very clear and easy to follow. This is the principal reason I'm so grateful for this book. I have a library of theological and psychological texts that have helped me to both find my way and to help others, but this is the book I will be presenting to people with confidence. Richard's counsel is easy to understand. He lovingly gives us the tools to dismantle the prison and build a future. Richard tells us what to do next.

My eyes have just fallen on Psalm 107:14 "He brought them out of darkness and deepest gloom and broke away their chains." Keep following Jesus, this testimony will also be yours.

– John Dawson
President Emeritus, Youth With A Mission

Introduction

> The body is not meant for sexual immorality,
> but for the Lord, and the Lord for the body.
> — 1 Corinthians 6:13b

> [Say to] the captives, "Come out," and to those
> in darkness, "Be free!"
> — Isaiah 49:9 NIV

For years, I lived a double life. Publicly, I was the leader of a Christian ministry telling others about God's love and how it could free them from all their brokenness. Privately, I was bound in my own chains, chasing momentary relief from unresolved pain in illicit sexual activity.

When it all finally came crashing down, there was actually a sense of relief. Being caught between what you want to believe and the way you actually live is exhausting. The shame never goes away. You try harder, as if you can somehow work off the guilt, but you never get there.

I'm not going to give you all the details of my wrongdoing here, but not because I'm trying to hide anything. The reason is that, especially when it comes to issues of sexual brokenness, we can all too easily get caught up in comparisons that keep us from finding freedom.

We may read someone's story and think, "Well, I was never as bad as that," and so we decide we don't really need to deal with our stuff because it's not so "serious." Or we may read someone's story and think, "I was so much worse than that," and so we decide that we are beyond hope. Either way, we remain stuck.

Just know that my sexual sin led to me forfeiting everything. My marriage. My relationship with my children, for a season. My leadership role. Yet, painful as all that was, today I can say that I am glad that my secret was exposed, because I am free at last.

And you can be, too! You don't have to be forever miserable and guilty, caught between wanting to serve God and feeling like you're letting Him down all the time.

If that's where you are, you are certainly not alone. In a teaching I heard, Benjamin Nolot, the founder of Exodus Cry, an organization fighting human trafficking, said that 70% of male congregants and 30-40% of women congregants in American churches use pornography on a regular basis—and so do 50% of pastors!

Apart from the personal shame and damaged relationships of the individuals involved, just think how sexual brokenness in the Church is keeping so many Christians from being the light to the world they are called to be.

God's Word is clear on what our standard should be. Read slowly what 1 Thessalonians 4:3-8 (NET) says, for example (I'm spacing, italicizing and underlining the verses to help you reflect thoughtfully on what may be familiar words):

> For this is *God's will*: that you become *holy*,
> that you *keep away* from sexual immorality,

that each of you *know* how to *possess*
[steward or control]

his own body
in holiness and honor,

<u>not</u> in lustful passion
like the Gentiles who do *not know God*.

In this matter no one should violate the rights
of his brother [or sister]

or *take advantage* of him [or her],
because the Lord is *the avenger* in all these cases,

as we also told you earlier and warned you solemnly.
For God did not call us to impurity
but in holiness.

Consequently *the one who rejects this* is not rejecting human authority
but God, who gives his Holy Spirit to you.

This is a serious calling, but I want you to know it is not out of reach. I have found it to be achievable since I faced the fact that I was a sex addict back in April 2011 and began to pursue freedom. I'm not pretending that I never face temptation, but I have learned how to deal with it. I have found that it is possible to overcome what seems to be the greatest personal struggle many people face. And as I have shared what I have discovered and experienced with others, they have been able to break free too.

I am not a professional counselor, but the principles I offer have been gleaned from many years of road-tested therapy, support group involvement, prayer, and personal study. I want to make what I have learned easily accessible. So I write as an average guy who got lost for a long time, as you may be, as someone who found his way home and who now wants to share the road map that has helped me and many others get on the right path. The journey isn't easy, it's not instant, it's not magical. However, by embracing some simple practices, you can find the healing and hope you may currently believe isn't achievable. I am walking proof!

Note that this is only possible if you really, really want it. And it's not something you can impose on other people: without someone's genuine desire to get free, it won't happen. But if you're ready to change, let me offer some tools that will help.

I have deliberately kept this book short. You can read it all the way through in less than a couple of hours, but I believe that if you are serious, it can help you set your life on a new course.

Goals and degrees

As we set out, I need to address two important points.

First, you need to have a clear goal in mind. Many people just want to be able to stop whatever unwanted behavior is affecting their lives. "If I can just get over this, then everything would be great!" they think. But that's shortsighted. There is a difference between being "sober" (not doing something) and being truly free.

Those problem behaviors are like the tip of an iceberg. They are what you can see above the waterline, but there is so much more below the surface. Simply tackling the 20% that may be visible leaves so much unaddressed. It's like taking medicine when you have a cold. You are not actually dealing with the issue—there's currently no cure for the common cold—you are only suppressing the symptoms.

You may melt the part of the iceberg that's above the waterline, but in time that which was below is going to bob to the surface to replace it. It's the same with sexual brokenness. We develop these patterns of behavior as a way of soothing unresolved pain—they become an almost predictable cycle (see the Understanding the Cycle of Addiction diagram in the appendices). We need to get to the roots of those hurts if we are to move beyond "sin management" to actual liberty. As is said in many support groups, it's not just about sobriety, it's about recovery and healing.

Second, you need to recognize that sexual issues are on a continuum. At one level, the greater freedom there is these days to talk about addiction issues—of any kind—is a good thing. But it can also be unhelpful, because the idea of "addiction" can be thrown around too easily.

Inappropriate sexual behavior seems to progress in stages, and it is important to know where you are so you can address your issues appropriately. Some counselors talk about habits, compulsions, and addictions.

Habits. We all develop them—ways of doing things that reduce the amount of time we have to think about them. They just become second nature—brushing our teeth, putting tomorrow's clothes out before you go to bed. Maybe turning to porn when we feel hurt. But these are all actions that we can unlearn or reprogram without a great deal of trouble, if we are shown how to.

Compulsions. These are habits that are hardening. It may not be quite as easy to stop the behavior as a habit, but with the right tools and some accountability, you can make the change. Sometimes people in this stage fear they are already "addicted," when they are not.

Addictions. This is where you have tried many times to stop and failed repeatedly. You are at the point where you are willing to sacrifice the things that are most important to you—your relationships, your reputation, your role—to get that fix of relief. It's serious—but even here, where I found myself, it is possible to change!

It's helpful to have a sense of where you stand because that will shape how you need to go about facing your issues. You wouldn't use a sledgehammer to knock a small nail into a wall so you could hang a picture. But you'd need to use more than a tack hammer if you want to demolish an interior wall to create a new living space. It's all about finding the appropriate tools. There are several free assessment checklists available online that can help you determine your level of "stuck." You will also find one (Assessing Your Situation) in the appendices to this book that can help.

Perhaps you need the encouragement of knowing that you're not an "addict," but that you can overcome those wrong behaviors that you know are holding you back. Or perhaps you need the wake-up call of acknowledging you are caught in addiction to galvanize you to want to get free. Wherever you are, you don't have to stay there.

The first step is getting honest. I had tried many times through my years of addiction to get free—inner healing, prayer for deliverance, confession, self-discipline, you name it. I had genuinely wanted to be free—but not at any cost. I'd never really, fully faced myself. I'd rationalized, minimized, excused, deflected.

Those "wonder cure" pharmaceutical ads in magazines usually have a lot of small print beneath the bright, happy pictures, don't they? All the details about why the medicine might not work and what the side effects could be.

Here's my small print: Adopting some of the practices and tools I share in the following pages can help you find freedom from your sexual struggles. But this is not a one-and-done exercise. It's rinse and repeat—an invitation to a whole new lifestyle. But it is so worth it!

SECTION ONE:
The Small Hammer
(Habit/Early Compulsion)

#1 – Be Brutally Honest

Total honesty and humility are always the path to full healing. That's why the first of the Twelve Steps that have helped so many break free from addiction is the admission that "we are powerless" over whatever has ensnared us. Only then can we hope to find a way out, because "God resists the proud, but gives grace to the humble" (1 Peter 5:5).

This confession has to be twofold. First, with yourself and with God, admitting that you really do have a problem. But you cannot keep this to yourself. Your enemy, the devil, wants to keep you as isolated as possible, believing you're the only one with this problem. He whispers, "If others really knew 'this' about you, then no one would love you!" But 1 John 1:7 says that "if we walk in the light, as he is in the light, we have fellowship with one another, and the blood of Jesus, his Son, purifies us from all sin."

Radical honesty means facing our shame. We'll look at this more closely later, but for now, it's just important to recognize that shame can hold us back from being real with people because we're so concerned about what they will think—but that fear is actually rooted in a form of pride. Conquering this temptation to stay in hiding is essential if you are going to get real freedom.

Having said that, you need to be cautious about who you choose to share with. Look for people who have some understanding of the issue you're dealing with—personally or pastorally. They don't necessarily have to be a professional, though meeting with someone who is trained will be advantageous at some stage.

Brutal honesty means sharing specifics. For many years, when people would ask me how I was doing in the area of purity, I'd answer something like, "Oh, pretty good!" But that was deliberately vague—it could mean that I hadn't acted out in the last couple of weeks, or maybe I had, but in a way that I felt less guilty about than some others.

Though I didn't realize it at the time, I was straight-up lying to myself so that I could sleep at night. After all, I was a ministry leader! So, I minimized, justified, and rationalized my behaviors as "not that bad" compared to what I could have done or even what others were doing.

It wasn't until I finally realized how serious my problem was that I was finally able to begin to be 100% honest—and even then, it took some practice. But as I did so, I found that, with nowhere to hide, the shame and guilt began to drop off. As the saying goes, "Sunlight is the best disinfectant." Commit to being 100% brutally honest with those that you can appropriately trust.

ACTION STEPS:

1. Begin by being 100% honest with yourself and the Lord. How bad is your condition? One of the definitions of the word *confession* in Scripture is to call something out in yourself in the way that God sees it—and remember, He sees it all!

Consider speaking all this out loud; it may feel a bit odd, but actually giving voice to your situation can help make it more real, somehow.

2. Who is God telling you to confess all this to? Make a list of people that you sense you are supposed to share this with and stay accountable to in this area.

3. Commit to being brutally honest. Don't just talk about having "messed up." Share the exact nature of your wrong and in enough detail to be absolutely clear. This is important as it will help you get fully free and lead you to discover where the roots of your issue are (more on that later).

#2 – Find Your Supporters

As I've said, having a small team of people to share with on a regular basis, whenever you are tempted, is the bottom line and may actually be the main key to healing and recovery. You simply cannot get free from an addiction, and most of the time from a compulsion, on your own. You need to get a community.

Make a list of at least five people with whom you have shared your situation and to whom you can turn whenever you're tempted, for prayer or a word of encouragement. Chances are not everyone will be able to respond immediately to a text, but at least one of them should. Let them know who else is part of this team, so you can group-text them, if need be.

My experience, and that of others, is that if you learn to do this, temptation is reduced instantly by as much as

80 percent. It's remarkably effective—but it's not easy. After all, who wants to reach out to someone and go into specific details of our temptations? But if you learn to do this in detail regularly, you will find a new freedom like never before

The apostle Paul provides us with a great example of the power of humility and vulnerability. In 2 Corinthians 12:10, he writes, "For the sake of Christ, then, I am content with weaknesses, insults, hardships, persecutions, and calamities. *For when I am weak, then I am strong*" (emphasis added).

Here Paul is being vulnerable and sharing an area of his life where he is completely weak. We don't know what he is exactly talking about—theologians have suggested that it was everything from depression to physical sickness (maybe something to do with his eyes) or even a troublesome wife—but whatever the issue, he is sharing something that probably has brought some shame into his life. It's something that God refuses to take away, saying, "My grace is sufficient for you, for my power is made perfect in weakness" (2 Corinthians 12;9). "Therefore," Paul continues, "I will boast all the more gladly of my weaknesses, so that the power of Christ may rest upon me" (v.10).

The Greek literally says, "My power comes to *full strength* in weakness"—in other words, when we are weak, we ARE strong! I believe that to experience that *full strength* we must do what Paul does in this passage: be vulnerable! When we share our weaknesses, then we get the full strength of God's power to not be weak any longer.

So, instead of acting out, we should reach out! In the sharing, the temptation lessens and God's power in us to resist comes to full strength. If we don't reach out, we're on our own, reliant on our own, limited strength, and the temptation remains the same.

Action Steps:

1. Ask people to be on your support team in this area. About five seems to work best, so that it's likely someone will always be available if you're feeling tempted. However, don't be discouraged if it's less than five to start with. It's better to begin with even just one or two than not to do this.

2. Try a "test run" text with them and ask them to be fully prepared to answer back each time, if possible.

3. If you feel particularly tempted, a phone call or a quick one-on-one meeting, if one of them is nearby, might be better.

4. Don't get discouraged if it feels awkward at first. It will get easier with time, I promise. So, stick with it!

#3 – Identify Your "Gates"

On a hike, you sometimes have to open and close gates along the way. So it is in acting out: we never just arrive at the end—we get there through a series of "gates" or situations (thoughts or feelings). If we can identify what these progressions are, we can stop the "hike to acting out" right there by humbly reaching out to someone and sharing where we are.

For example, suppose the arrival point on your "hike," Gate 5, is looking at pornography and masturbating. If so, reflect on what typically happens right before that. What are the gates you have passed through on your way here—your thoughts and feelings, the circumstances? As you do this, you may discover that Gate 4 is most commonly when you are alone in a room with your phone and feeling tempted to look at stuff that is arousing.

Then, as you press in more to the Lord, ponder your pattern, and retrace your steps, you discover that before that, your Gate 3 is most commonly feeling lonely. Well, where did that come from? Oh, wait: Gate 2 is often feeling some kind of rejection from people you are close to. Maybe it was the day before, when you weren't invited to that party? Then, as you continue to review the way things often go, you realize that your Gate 1 is when you haven't been very connected to God in your devotional times.

Note that this process will be completely different for each individual—and some may pass through more "gates" than others. But once you have identified your series of gates, rather than waiting until you're super-tempted at Gate 4—right before you usually act out—you can begin to reach out sooner

Let's say feeling lonely is your Gate 3: when you recognize you have reached it, you can reach out to your text group: "Guys, I'm not tempted yet, but I know I'm feeling lonely right now and this usually leads to me acting out later on to 'kill the pain 'of this. So, I'm reaching out now in humility: please pray for me, that I avoid any temptation that may come later!"

One young man who I worked with who has gained sobriety and freedom through working this program recognized that his Gate 2 or Gate 3 was getting sick. Whenever he would start feeling ill in any way, he would begin to get annoyed. To kill the pain of that, he would go on Snapchat or Instagram and into chat rooms and ask random girls for nude pictures, and then sometimes he sent pictures of himself to them.

As he entered into recovery and put these tools into practice, he learned to share when he was feeling ill with his group chat and ask for support and prayer. As a result, he found that most of the time he never reached the point of temptation because he had humbled himself before there was even a chance for it to take a hold of him.

ACTION STEPS:

Pray and journal to discern what your "gates" are. This may take some time to do, and you may want to add to them or adjust them later, but it's an important process. It's helpful to "retrace" your steps backward from arrival at Gate 5.

> Gate 5: Acting out (what is "acting out" for you?).

> Gate 4: This is right before you most commonly act out: What are the common places, situations, thoughts, feelings, and emotions in these times of temptation? Who or what are you thinking of?

Gate 3: These could be triggering thoughts, feelings, people, places, even smells (which are strongly tied to our memories and emotions). Oftentimes, these are not situations or circumstances that you have sought out but which you find yourself in unintentionally. However, they provoke reactions and responses in us that lead to the temptation to act out. If unaddressed, these triggers can lead to frustrations and obsessive thoughts that lead us to Gate 4.

Gate 2: Similar to Gate 3, but maybe less impacting, these are incidents, situations, or feelings that, unchecked, can lead to the more intense things that we can't let go of at Gate 3. Common issues are sickness or unpleasant situations or circumstances that create some kind of anxiety.

Gate 1: Here we're dealing with things that don't seem especially concerning but are part of the ongoing, unpleasant "background noise" in our lives—things that irritate us a little when we think about them, but we don't dwell on them much. They might include financial concerns, not eating well, lack of sleep, or not paying enough attention to our spiritual well-being. As a result, we can find ourselves not loving ourselves enough—or others, or God.

#4 – Don't Go There

If you want to stop drinking, that usually means you need to quit going to bars. Likewise, in the area of sexual wholeness, you have to stay away from your sources of arousing material, locations, or triggers. For most people, that immediately means limiting access to the internet, or certain websites or apps. Thankfully, these days there are settings on your devices that can restrict access either in terms of maximum minutes used or certain times of the day.

I know a large number of guys who have struggled in this area late at night or first thing in the morning who have enlisted a roommate to lock access to the internet or other potentially "dangerous" apps on their phones before 9 a.m. or after 9 p.m., which is often when they are most vulnerable. For many, this simple step might be all that they need to find significant freedom.

Another option is to remove all devices from your room at certain vulnerable times of the day. Leave them in the living room or give them to your friends or parents. Now, this won't deal with the heart motivation or roots of the problem, of course, but it will get you to the place of not acting out and will provide the relief and "sober thinking" that you need to be able to find the heart of the issue.

Sometimes we may have to be even more radical, though, like a friend of mine I'll call Nathan. For him, masturbation in the shower had become a compulsion he simply couldn't stop. So, he decided he needed to get really serious about it.

While showering, he left the dorm door to his bathroom unlocked, and if he got tempted while he was soaping up, he would call for his trusted friend, Josh, to come and be in the room while he was showering, just to make sure that he would not take things any further.

A little awkward, for sure, but that kind of radical humility works! What are you willing to give up to get free? Inconvenience? No access to phones? People knowing that you're weak? Some privacy?

A quick footnote here: Whatever decision you make in this area usually needs to be discussed, agreed upon, and committed to with someone *beforehand*. This should be your main accountability person or "sponsor," the one who is mostly your coach or mentor through this process. This will keep you on track and make sure that you're not making wild commitments that you can never follow through on.

ACTION STEPS:

1. Pray and make a list of what you need to limit access to. What media do you need to cut off, either completely or in private? You still may be able to look at social media, for example, but do you need to make a commitment not to access it in private? For instance, some people decide never to take any devices into the bathroom.

2. Once you have decided what you need to do, check in with your sponsor first and write it down so that you can both see it, so that clear accountability is established.

#5 – Get Yourself Grounded

If you're feeling particularly tempted to act out or you find yourself stuck in an unhelpful place of fantasy that you don't want to be in, you can break the pull by practicing "grounding." This involves using one of the five senses God has given you to help interrupt your current train of thought. Sight probably isn't the best one to choose, as we can get so easily distracted, so maybe pick hearing or touch.

Let's try this with touch. Close your eyes and touch the seat that you're sitting on. Focus. What does it feel like? Rough or smooth? Is there soft material or a hard surface? What's it made of? Think about it for a couple of seconds... and, voila! You have stopped thinking about whatever it was that you were so focused on before.

The next level for this is to then focus on Jesus. Think about what He is like: His character, His personality. How does He feel about you? Focus on how, through the cross, He has set you free from every sin and brokenness. If you're able to do this, it really does bring breakthrough from distracting or intrusive thoughts.

I have found great benefit in "The 123 Prayer" my former sponsor taught me. It's based on the first three steps of the 12 Step program. It starts in the same way I just outlined above, where you get quiet and center yourself on Jesus, but then you do the following:

Tell Him that you can't resist sin, temptation, or fantasy on your own without Him.

Declare that He is God and He is able to help you and set you free.

Give Him whatever you are facing in that moment, knowing that He is not only able to take it and deal with it, but also that He actually wants to!

Action Steps:

1. Pick one or all of these ideas and try them out *before you are tempted.* Rehearse them before you need them, so that you are ready and know what to do when you are tempted.

2. Decide which one works best for you and have it ready when you need it.

#6 – Seek Prayer Ministry

This may seem very obvious, and for many of us it's probably the first thing that we do—and that's good! But why doesn't it always work? Why can't we just "pray away" our problems, as they say? There are many reasons for this, but let me list a few of the most common ones:

- There's the matter of degree. If you're dealing with an ingrained problem, it often takes more than a few simple prayers—and even a few powerful ones!

- The issue may be deeply rooted, because sexuality is often strongly related to our core identity. When we are in our mom's womb, we get the genitalia that determine our sexual identity at week nine. It's one of the first things that makes us who we are after we receive our major organs—and at less than 25% of our development. Thus, when things go wrong or we receive some unwanted imprinting because of things done to us, or unhealthy things that we have done, we can be affected in some of our deepest parts.

- Studies of brain scans of people experiencing an orgasm or on a crack/cocaine "high" have found many similarities. The amounts of dopamine and other euphoric chemicals that flood our brains in those moments are intense and addictive; that's why we often want to experience them again, and it can be so hard to stop once we open that "Pandora's Box"!

- According to the Word of God, the main way that we are transformed is by the renewing of our minds. In Romans 12:1-2, Paul writes:

I appeal to you therefore, brothers, by the mercies of God, to present your bodies as a living sacrifice, holy and acceptable to God, which is your spiritual worship. Do not be conformed to this world, but be transformed by the renewal of your mind, that by testing you may discern what is the will of God, what is good and acceptable and perfect.

This process usually takes time, but I promise you it's worth it.

By all means, receive as much prayer in "ministry times" and personally as possible, and with that, some specific deliverance ministry, if necessary. If we continue to willfully sin as believers, we can open ourselves up to being affected by demonic forces and we may need to get prayer from other believers to be set free from them.

Look for someone who is experienced in this area to pray with you. You may also need inner healing prayer for traumatic past memories that may have caused some unresolved pain that might be part of the roots of your unwanted behaviors. Again, be sure to look for someone who is experienced in this area.

Action Steps:

1. If you've been putting off either getting prayer for inner healing or deliverance prayer, reach out and make an appointment today with someone that you trust.

2. During your next prayer gathering or small group meeting, ask for prayer along these lines with those around you that you trust. Don't be afraid of doing this often and being persistent (as long as you are using the other tools in this book and are playing your part where you need to—other people's prayers are a supplement to our own efforts, not a substitute for them).

#7 – Count the Cost

Spend some quality time thinking about what might happen to you if you act out. Remember, you will avoid that possibly costly consequence by not acting out! What are you seeking to avoid by pursuing sobriety? Write these scenarios down and get them into your head, so you can remind yourself of them if and when you're tempted.

For example, what could happen if you continue with this behavior? Might you lose close relationships that are important to you? Or what about your job, is that at risk? I wish I could say that just thinking about the hurt and grieving that we cause the Holy Spirit within us would be enough to stop us from inappropriate behavior with our minds or bodies, but, unfortunately, most of us pass by that thought really fast. After a while, we can even begin to believe it's not that big of a deal as so many others are doing it.

So that they can sleep at night and still function in their everyday lives, many addicts and compulsives operate in what's called "The Major" (The MJR). They:

Minimize how bad the problem is: "If I tried really hard enough, I could stop anytime!" (So why don't you, then?)

Justify how bad the problem is: "Well, everyone else is doing it, too; it's so common for someone my age to struggle with this. Therefore, it's okay to the point that I don't really have to do anything different to change it." (Our standard of holiness should be based on what God says, not what other people do.)

Rationalize how bad the problem is: "I'm not really hurting anyone else, except maybe God . . . I'm just blowing off some steam and stress: work/life/ministry is really stressful." (So it's okay to hurt God?)

Within the last year of writing this book, more Christian leaders have either confessed to or been caught out in moral failures than at any other time in my life. "How did this happen?" people have asked. How were these leaders able to continue in ministry, knowing what they were up to? As someone who, like them, lived a double life for years, I can tell you the primary answer: The MJR! Many addiction recovery groups believe that this is one of the greatest characteristics of its members: that they can end up justifying almost any wrong behavior and make it sound reasonable to themselves.

So, we need to come to terms with how serious things are, but also just how much more serious things will become if we don't pursue the help that we need to get free. Thinking about this and rehearsing it when we are not being tempted helps us in times of actual temptation to not act out, knowing that the consequences that we face will be real.

ACTION STEPS:

Write down the answers to the following questions: seeing them in black and white makes them harder to minimize or dismiss.

1. If I continue to act out, who will I hurt? God? Me? My spouse? My kids? My future spouse or kids? Future generations?

2. If I continue to act out, might I get arrested, or possibly have my health affected in some way?

3. If I continue to act out, will I, or even should I, be able to stay in my current job (or role of serving in my church or ministry)?

4. If I continue to act out, how will this affect or might this affect those that I am leading or seeking to disciple?

5. Are there any other negative effects that I need to consider and write down as deterrents to acting out?

#8 – Avoid Your Triggers

An emotional trigger can be almost anything that reminds you of some "pain" or trauma that you underwent in the past that creates a level of discomfort in you, to the point that you are then tempted to "remove" or numb it by acting out in an unhealthy way. The trigger can be something seemingly random: a thought or memory, a scent or a smell, something seen (a piece of clothing), or something heard (a comment from someone, or even a piece of music).

A sexual trigger is when someone who fits our "attraction template" walks by, or we see them in a movie, or a picture, and our brain is triggered to want to meet that arousal or need for intimacy in an unhealthy way.

Triggers are perfectly normal—you can't expect to go through life without experiencing them. But, as with temptation (which comes as a result of them), we are responsible for managing our response to them in a healthy and godly way. How do we do this? Here's some tips and tricks:

- Avoid places where you know that you will be tempted! Just like an alcoholic can never go into a bar again, what, who, or where is your "never again"? Are you willing to do whatever it takes?

- Don't try to negotiate with temptation; run from it! 1 Corinthians 6:18 is pretty direct: "Flee from sexual immorality." As Joseph fled when Potiphar's wife came on to him, just get out of there.

It's important to do the work of identifying your triggers through prayer and journaling so that you are aware in advance of what they are and so that you can be ready and know what to do when they happen. If you have a formal sponsor (from some kind of recovery group) or a mentor or a coach in this area, you should discuss these triggers with them and agree on a prearranged course of action if they occur. They can then hold you accountable in this area so that you don't lie to yourself.

Action Steps:

1. Pray and list your emotional triggers. When you discover new ones, you can add them later. Seek healing for them by following other tools listed in this book.

2. Pray and list your sexual triggers here. Know what they are and do everything that you can to avoid them. Predetermine to "run" from them if they present themselves to you.

3. Share both of these lists with someone that you trust, if you feel comfortable doing so, and let them know what you plan to do about them.

#9 – Recruit Extra Help

While your "core" team of five or so confidants is your first line of defense or protection, it can be helpful to recruit additional supporters. These are people with whom you have some level of trust—maybe friends or even coworkers—who you might ask for help in "achieving your goals." You don't have to go into the same kind of detail you have with those others, but you can ask them in appropriate ways to keep you accountable.

For example, you could tell them that you're really trying to grow in character areas of your life, striving to be a "better man/woman," or seeking to be a better follower of Jesus, and so you'd like to ask them, for instance, to help you not waste time on social media. Invite them to point it out if they see you alone with your phone, or to ask how much time you've spent on social media recently. Most people will be only too happy to help and won't consider you odd for asking—in fact, they may even be challenged personally by what you're seeking to do. This adds another level of accountability in those everyday situations.

Action Steps:

1. Pray and ask God to guide you as to who you should ask to help you with this.

2. Evaluate how helpful this tool is to you and adjust as needed.

#10 – Reset for Ninety

According to many brain specialists, there is good news—an old dog can learn new tricks! It used to be thought that after the age of 25, there was not a lot of hope for changed behavior, once one's prefrontal cortex had fully developed.

However, in recent years, after many studies, experts have discovered that even later on in life we can change our behaviors if we want to, because the brain is more like plastic than stone. Rather than being set or stuck in its old patterns, it can learn new ways.

This shouldn't really be a surprise to Christians—after all, as I noted earlier, in Romans 12:2, Paul exhorts us not to be conformed to the ways of the world, "but be transformed by the renewing of your mind." The Greek word *metamorphoo* is where we get the term metamorphosis from, like a caterpillar transforming into a totally different creature, the butterfly.

According to brain specialists, if you are able to stop a certain behavior for up to somewhere between 63-90 days, then at that point your brain "resets," so that whatever that habit or behavior was, it is now possible to change it. Some people have experienced the reality of this through taking on a 90-day challenge to abstain from unwanted sexual behavior, and they have seen an incredible breakthrough that they never thought possible.

In fact, there is even a movement in secular circles among young men who have chosen to pursue freedom from masturbation and pornography just because they are so sick of it and, while not religious, they recognize how it has been stripping away their masculinity and, even, their humanity.

ACTION STEPS:

1. Pray and decide before the Lord if this is something that you should try and pursue.

2. Pray and create a list of people that you need to share this with for accountability and support.

3. For more information about how to reset your neural pathways, you can always get lots more information from people such as Dr Caroline Leaf (www.drleaf.com), through her books and podcasts.

...

If you have tried using the above tools for some time and you are still not feeling that you have seen the breakthrough that you want to see, then it's time to start adding some more.

So, if this is you, that's okay, but we're gonna need a bigger hammer!

SECTION TWO:
The Medium-Sized Hammer
(Middle-to Late-Compulsion to Early Addiction)

#11 - Understand Your Circles

It was super-hard for me to admit that I really did have a sexual addiction problem because I was in so much denial, but when I did, my counselor required me to join a Sex Addicts Anonymous group. It was here I was introduced to a system that, over time, can help you achieve sobriety and freedom from acting out. In it, you identify what is called your Three Circles of Sobriety, or Addiction:

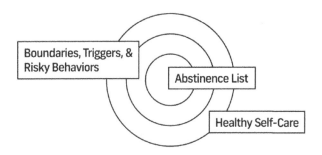

In the Inner circle is your "Abstinence List"—these are the Gate 5 things that you absolutely do not want to do anymore. If you do these things, then you must acknowledge that you have "lost your sobriety." And remember, we want to stay "sober" so that we are no longer "drunk" or numbed out by our unhealthy behavior, so that we can find the roots of our issues and pull them up.

Now, this needs to be "do-able," so that we can get and maintain our sobriety as quickly as possible, so the best approach is to not put everything that we no longer want to do in this circle, but rather the things that we most desperately want to stop.

Don't try to take on everything all at once, because it will be overwhelming. It's a bit like getting out of debt—the experts recommend you concentrate on paying off one credit card at a time, so you get a "win" and gain some traction. So, it's probably best to limit this Inner circle list to maybe three or four things. Set too high a bar and you are likely to end up failing and feeling defeated. We're looking for progress, not perfection

For instance, visiting massage parlors and having anonymous sex, or looking at pornography and masturbating, would need to be on this list, but glancing at the magazine covers at the supermarket checkout may not. Don't get me wrong, we're not saying that is okay, or acceptable, but one thing at a time! We need to put out the fire before redoing all the wiring in the house.

The Middle circle activities ("Boundaries, Triggers, and Risky Behaviors") may well be wrong and still need to be confessed as sin to Jesus and to those that you are walking with, but if you act on these you will not "lose your sobriety."

Viewing these things somewhat more lightly—at least, for now—should not be confused with dismissing them. These actions should act as alarm bells to us that we are in danger of losing our sobriety. They are not "okay," and we are going to address them in due course. It can be tempting to "camp out" here because we pride ourselves on the fact that we are not "losing our sobriety," while in actuality we're giving ourselves a pass to do things that are a little edgy. If we are not careful, we can turn what should be a "grace area" into a "license area." Don't fool yourself: if we continue in these areas for any length of time, they will end up leading us into Inner circle behaviors, so watch out!

The Outer circle is for anything healthy that takes us away from acting out: Prayer and worship; reading the Word of God and other helpful books; being with friends; going on a hike; engaging with positive media, sports, art, and entertainment; doing a good day's work; and so on. The goal is to stay and live in this Outer circle, because it is the most loving thing we can do—for both ourselves and for others.

ACTION STEPS:

1. Identify and write down your three circles so that they are clear in your mind and share them with those who have agreed to help hold you accountable in these areas, which means at least your sponsor or coach.

2. Seek their input on what goes in your Inner and Middle circles; ask them to help you determine whether you are being too religious or restrictive, setting unrealistic goals, or conversely being too easy and giving yourself too much "wiggle room."

3. Be prepared to adapt these over time. The goal is that, as you grow in healing, strength, and wisdom your Middle circle will shrink and your Inner circle will grow.

#12 – Establish Real Consequences

Most of us have continued in our unhealthy ways because we have never really had to pay the price for those poor choices. For me, that meant the habit I developed when I was young became a compulsion and then an addiction. When I fell in love with the woman who would become my wife, I didn't act out for the whole time of our dating and engagement, and into the first two years of marriage. I told myself that I was free, hallelujah!

But, unfortunately, big issues in our lives never just "go away" by themselves. They are like the iceberg I mentioned earlier. The part that is above the waterline may melt away, but there's much more below that will rise to the surface. If we don't deal with the roots, something is going to emerge eventually. Just hoping that things will get better over time is not a strategy!

I came to realize that while on a ministry speaking tour of the West Coast of the United States. On my journey home, I acted out. Though I was, of course, fully responsible for what I did, at the same time, I was in shock: How could this be? I thought I was free. Now what should I do?

I was too afraid to tell my wife, and my shame was just off the charts. So, I decided to seek help from two gifted counselors who were part of the ministry I was serving with at the time. They were very kind and sympathetic as they heard my story but, unfortunately, they ended up giving me what, in hindsight, I realize was some bad counsel. "Don't tell your wife," they advised. "She will find it hard to understand." Wow: a massive flood of relief filled my mind and body. I'd dodged the bullet! Now I had another chance to not do this again... or so I thought.

Of course, the trouble was that the exact opposite happened: because there was no obvious consequence for my actions in my primary, God-given covenant relationship, it meant that I could now do anything! I had taken what was meant as grace and mercy (although obviously misguided) and turned it into a "hall pass," a license to do anything. Sadly, over the next 15 years of my marriage, I acted out anywhere between three and 11 times a year, betraying my wife horribly.

Healthy fear is good. It keeps most of us from doing silly things, like handstands on the edge of a high cliff. In the same way, godly boundaries and consequences truly are His gift to us. So, a great tool to help you from acting out in your area of brokenness is to talk to your sponsor/coach and decide together what would be a good consequence that you can set up that would act as a deterrent to make you think at least twice before you act out.

For example, who do you not want to know about your issue? Your spouse, your mom, your girlfriend or boyfriend, your boss? Might you lose your role or position if you continue in this or don't improve, and it is made known? The most effective real consequences involve some sort of disclosure or exposure to people who are important to us, and which may have some impact on our relationship with them.

This sounds kind of harsh, but it's a measure of how committed you really are to dealing with what you are facing. And it underscores the seriousness with which you need to identify the person you want to ask to be your primary accountability contact. Are they willing to lovingly hold your feet to the fire, to keep you accountable for what you have said?

Action Steps:

1. Through prayer and counsel with your sponsor/coach, determine what are the most effective consequences that will help you stop your unwanted behavior. This may take some time.

2. Make sure that you're not being too extreme (or too lenient) in setting these consequences.

3. If you find this consequence doesn't work, then you need to step up the agreed-upon ramification to something a little more challenging.

#13 – Make Contingency Plans

Have you ever wondered why flight attendants keep going through the same boring in-case-of-emergency instructions for passengers over and over again? Why don't they just gather all the first-time fliers together and tell them what to do if something bad happens during the flight? Why are hotels required by law to have a little map on the back of every room's door, detailing the way to the emergency exit? It's so that, if something bad should happen and a fire breaks out, you know where to go and what to do so you won't die!

Why is it, then, that we think that when we're tempted by something— particularly in an area of sexual brokenness where we have a history of failing, and which has the potential to create a debilitating addiction for our whole lives—that we think we have no need of a planned way of escape, that somehow we can just wing it in the moment?

When you ask a soldier what they do when in combat, they will always say that their training takes over. All those drills prepare them to know what to do without having to think about it. And yet for many of us (particularly as Jesus-followers), we somehow seem to think that it's God's job to look after us in that moment of extreme stress or temptation. "It's okay: I'll cross that bridge when I come to it!"

No: We have to be prepared! Like the flight attendants, we need to rehearse in advance what we are going to do should a certain situation arise. This has been called making "pre-decisions."

We see in the Bible that, in taking care of sin, God treats it seriously and makes it our responsibility to deal with it! In Genesis 4, when Cain's offering is rejected by

God—almost certainly because of a bad attitude in his giving, and a lack of faith and worship in his behavior— He doesn't destroy him immediately but rather He warns him and calls him to some personal responsibility. In Genesis 4:6-7 (NIV, emphasis added), we read:

> Then the Lord said to Cain, "Why are you angry? Why is your face downcast? If you do what is right, will you not be accepted? But if you do not do what is right, *sin is crouching at your door; it desires to have you, but you must rule over it.*"

If we really want to get free, we really have to take things seriously and set up clear escape routes and rehearse and practice these contingency plans over and over. For example, what are you going to do the next time you find yourself alone in your room at night, bored or lonely or hurt, and you start doomscrolling on your phone, knowing how this is going to play out? You decide now that, when that happens, you will text or call a friend, get up and go out, or put your phone away somewhere.

This is such a simple and logical tool to use, yet so often we can miss this wonderful opportunity and way of escape.

Action Steps:

1. Write down 5-10 common scenarios for you where you have been tempted to act out inappropriately in the past.

2. Now, plan out what series of steps you will take the next time you face one of them. Write down these "pre-decisions" clearly and go over them in your mind.

3. Go a step further and actually act out the different positive steps that you will take differently, to build some actual "muscle memory" into your life.

4. Share these with your sponsor and your accountability crew so that they can help you identify any loopholes or "get-out" clauses you may have missed, and then hold you to these alternatives to acting out inappropriately.

#14 – Understand Your Pain

Pain is an inevitable part of life in a fallen world. We can't avoid it, though many of us try—that's how and why we find ourselves mired in compulsive behaviors and addiction! But the good news is we are not alone in having to face it. Here is Jesus's promise:

> "I have told you these things so that in me you may have peace. In the world you have trouble and suffering, but take courage—I have conquered the world." – John 16:33 (NET)

The Greek word in the Bible for "trouble and suffering" is thlîpsis. The best description of its meaning I have found is by Ron Lee Davis:

It may be cancer or a sore throat. It may be the illness or loss of someone close to you. It may be a personal failure or disappointment in your job or school work. It may be a rumor that is circulating in your office or your church, damaging your reputation, bringing you grief and anxiety. It can be anything that ranges from something as small and irritating as the bite of a mosquito to facing a lion in the lions' den as did Daniel (Dan. 6).[1]

Each of us has varying degrees of pain in different areas. Anxiety produces its own kind of pain or discomfort in our lives, for example, and so we end up finding ways to deal with that pain in unhealthy ways. For you, the issue may be boredom, hunger, anger, loneliness, tiredness, rejection, loss of control, various abuses you have suffered, emptiness, sexual arousal, temptation, or shame. How have you sought to soothe these "pains" until now?

We need to understand exactly what our "pains" are. Journal about them, pray into the issue and ask God for revelation and insight. Invite people who are close to you to share what they might think are your greatest points of "trouble," as Jesus put it. When you know what these issues are, then you can pursue healing in all of these areas. This is a serious undertaking. Be conscious that it's possible to do this work in a half-hearted way and then we wonder why we haven't found full freedom.

---

[1] *Gold in the Making: Where is God When Bad Things Happen to You?* by Ron Lee Davis (Thomas Nelson, 1984)

Action Steps:

1. Think, pray, and journal: what are the exact natures of your most common "pains"?

2. Run your thoughts about all this by the truth-tellers in your life—trusted friends, those who will not be tempted to sugarcoat your issues but rather "speak the truth in love" to you. Do they confirm or affirm what you think? Do you need to add or take away some of them?

3. Remember that God doesn't always want to take away all of these pains as quickly as we might like. But He does want to sit with us in them and have us share them with Him so that He can deal with them in a healthy way.

#15 – Study Your Sickness

It doesn't matter whether you call your issue a compulsion, an addiction, or just a problem—however you describe it, you need to study it and understand how it works and how to deal with it. Viewing your challenge as a sickness can be helpful—it's not something you are responsible for causing, but it is something you have a responsibility to deal with appropriately.

Let's take Type-2 diabetes as an example. If we were to meet someone with this sickness, we would have compassion for them, and hopefully we would never ridicule them for having a potentially deadly disease. Most of the time, it appears that there may be a propensity towards getting this disease from one's family history, but bad choices in the area of food and a lack of exercise can heighten the chances of developing it. It's like a partnership between our heredity and our choices.

The same is true for many of us who have an area of sexual brokenness. Parents or family members may have a history of addiction that has been passed down to us, but then we end up acting upon it, and now we have joined the chain of generational sin with them. We can break that spiritually through prayer, but we still will have to deal with the consequences that we may have brought upon ourselves in our own lives. You cannot just wish away your family's predisposition to developing diabetes, but once you know it is there, there are things in your power you can do to avoid that happening, like watching your diet and exercising.

So, we need to understand the exact nature of our condition to get healing. Ignorance is not bliss, it is bondage! Many people, even devout Jesus-followers, as I was, can be unnecessarily bound for years because they do not understand their situation.

To begin with, it's important to do some reading on the subject. To get started, I recommend two books by Patrick Carnes, a longtime counselor and respected expert in the area of sex addiction, *Out of the Shadows: Understanding Sexual Addictions* and *Don't Call it Love!: Recovery From Sexual Addiction*. Both of these can be tough to read because they are pretty graphic, and sometimes the detailed stories can be quite triggering.

These are not "Christian" books, and each is influenced to some degree by some secular humanism, but the honesty and rawness of them is often exactly what is needed to break the denial that many of us have kept in place for years. I ask everyone who joins one of my support groups to read these books because it's a bit like looking in the mirror—something many of us, because of shame, have not done before. We have to get brutally honest about exactly where we are at and how serious our issues are, if we are truly to begin the journey to freedom

Should either of these titles prove to be too triggering, I recommend a Christian book that covers the essential material but not quite as impactfully, in my opinion, Michael John Cusick's *Surfing for God: Discovering the Divine Desire Behind Sexual Struggle.*

ACTION STEPS:

1. Buy a copy of *Out of the Shadows* by Patrick Carnes and begin underlining all of the passages where you see yourself. Then do the same with the second book.

2. If this is really too triggering, then check out Michael John Cusick's book and do the same thing.

3. Make notes, process, and journal what you discover about yourself and what you need to do to pursue your healing pathway ahead.

#16 – Attend a Group

God intends for us to live in community, just as He lives in community in the Trinity. Not independently, where you don't need anyone, ever, nor co-dependently, where you can't live without each other, but rather in a healthy interdependency—where we have free will as an individual, but also choose to mutually submit to each other for help and accountability.

When we discover brokenness in any area of our lives, we can try to solve it on our own, "just me and God," but most of the time this doesn't work. One reason for that is, more often than not this is an expression of pride, because we just don't want to humble ourselves and share our issues with others. But we know that "God opposes the proud but gives grace to the humble" (1 Peter 5:5; James 4:6).

This means that when we confess our brokenness to Him and to others when we need to, He rushes in to help us deal with that very issue. Also, James 5:16 says: "Therefore, confess your sins to one another and pray for one another, that you may be healed." This is essential if we want to grow in Jesus, and especially in any areas of brokenness and weakness, as to do so breaks the power of shame in our lives as we walk in humility.

Sometimes, though, even when we do this, we can use what we call "half measures"—we're sort of honest, but not brutally so, because we are just too ashamed. But brutal honesty leads to deeper and faster freedom, because it brings a greater death to stuff. Consequently, we need to find a place that exists to deal with this issue in our lives, and that's going to be a formal recovery group of some kind.

At first, attending such groups can feel awkward, as our pride is hurt and our shame kicks into overdrive because now we are "one of those desperate people."

Yes, but if we really need help, isn't being desperate to be free and more like Jesus a good thing? And for some it's a huge relief to find people who can understand them without judgment, and they finally begin to discover solutions that they have been looking for, maybe for years.

These formal groups are different to the group of friends you may have recruited to be your accountability partners and supporters. These friends have your best interests at heart, but they may not really understand what you are dealing with in a deep way, and that's okay. They have their role to play. But members of formal groups bring something else to your recovery as people who have "been there and done that" and learned how not to!

You can go online and probably find a Sex Addicts Anonymous group or something similar that meets nearby. There are Christian versions of such groups (such as Celebrate Recovery). In my experience, these Christian groups can sometimes feel a little more diluted when you may need a more straight-up, "in your face" approach to shake you out of your denial. Just make sure that your pride is being truly challenged, otherwise your recovery won't be as deep.

I firmly recommend attending in-person meetings. Online gatherings can be beneficial, but physically sitting in a room with others can be so much more helpful because shame is broken off more effectively in person. Through a screen we are more able to save face, somehow.

Also, when you go to one of these meetings, remember that it's not just about what you receive. It's also important to share about your recovery, both the successes and failures, as it will help others. Be open, share, and listen!

Sometimes, when people really want to focus on jump-starting or a making a fresh recommitment to their recovery, they commit to a "90 for 90"—attending a recovery group every day for three months. This is similar to the 90-Day Reset mentioned previously, but even more seriously focused.

At the end of the day, we have to ask ourselves how much do we really want to get free? Are we *really* willing to do whatever it takes? If rewiring our brains ("being transformed by the renewing of our minds") is the primary goal—which it should be—this might be a key solution to get started.

Action Steps:

1. Go to https://saa-recovery.org/meetings/. This will show you the nearest Sex Addicts Anonymous meeting.

2. If you'd prefer a more Christian version you can search at https://crgroups.info. Make sure that this group is led by good and experienced people, so it will be effective for you. Ask God to guide you in your decision.

3. Commit to following through. Regular attendance at such groups is a truly effective key for freedom, even though it may be inconvenient and humbling!

#17 – Get a Sponsor

Once you have found a formal recovery group you are able to attend in person at least weekly, if possible, you should seek out a sponsor or a coach there to directly help with your healing and recovery.

This is someone in addition to whoever may be the main contact in your informal group of friends and supporters. This person is there to walk you through all of your recovery process. If you act out or are tempted, or just not sure what to do next, they are there as your guide to direct you to whatever is "the next right thing" to do. They will become your greatest ally, so choose wisely; you'll want to be sure you have the same worldview. At the same time, don't wait for the "perfect person" to come along before you jump in; you can always switch to someone else, if you need to. Not every sponsor will be a good fit for you, so if you're not connecting after a few meetings, feel free to change to one that is a better fit for you. They are there to serve you and so they shouldn't be offended by that. It happens.

What makes for a good sponsor? They will be someone who has gone through/is going through recovery and healing of sexual addiction or brokenness and understands what has happened to them and how the process of freedom works. They will have walked in significant freedom for a considerable amount of time and can help guide and serve others sacrificially through their own process of recovery. They are not perfect, but they are authentic, and they will share their failings with those that they are helping when appropriate and necessary.

You should seek to share every detail with your

sponsor. Meet with and talk with them at least once a week, sometimes more frequently if you get some specific revelation of growth, or there is something you particularly need to process. And if you act out in any way or need to discuss a change of what goes into each of your "circles," you will want to contact your sponsor first before the others in your recovery team, so that there is support and accountability.

Action Steps:

1. Don't wait too long before you ask someone to be your sponsor. At the end of most meetings, someone will commonly ask, "Who here is willing to be a sponsor?" and some will raise their hands.

2. Pick one and set up a first meeting with them.

3. Make sure that they have a similar worldview and values to you, otherwise it's unlikely that this will be of benefit to you.

4. Jump in! Commit to meeting and having regular contact with them and they will help you grow into freedom.

#18 – Face Your Shame

We are never going to experience true freedom without facing our shame, but it's a slippery thing to get to grips with. One dictionary definition of shame is "a painful feeling of humiliation or distress caused by the consciousness of wrong or foolish behavior." What does that look like in our everyday lives? Psychiatrist Peter Breggin lists some of shame's attributes in his book *Guilt, Shame, and Anxiety: Understanding and Overcoming Negative Emotions*:

- feeling worthless
- worrying what others think about you
- being afraid to look stupid
- perfectionism in response to fearing failure
- constant negative self-talk
- anger in response to shame triggers

Essentially, shame is when you just never feel like you're "enough," either in specific areas that you're aware of, or just generally. Unfortunately, if it's not dealt with, shame can bleed into every area of your life, so that you begin to believe that you are, in fact, "less than" everybody else. It can also express itself in self-hatred and the belief, "If only I could be better, then others would finally love me, but until that happens, I am just not fully acceptable."

One of the tricky things about the way shame operates, which makes it worse, is that it hides itself from us so that we can't deal with it. This is well illustrated in an episode of the long-running sci-fi TV series *Dr. Who*, about a time traveler.

In it, The Doctor, as he is known, goes back to the 1960s and discovers ugly, scary aliens living among us who want to take over the planet. They have an amazingly successful defense mechanism that keeps them undetected—as soon as anyone catches even so much as a glimpse of them, he or she immediately looks away in horror because the sight is so grotesque. In doing so, the person instantly forgets what they saw, leaving the aliens free to operate unhindered, continuing in their dastardly plan to take over Earth!

This is exactly how shame can operate in our lives. When we finally get a glimpse of our weaknesses and brokenness—which we must face, if we are to get free—shame comes and kicks us in the butt. We begin to feel so much pain and self-hatred that we can't bear it, so we look away and begin to use "The Major" (see tool seven)—we minimize, we justify, and we rationalize to forget what we have seen.

So, what must we do? We have to be brave and gear up for this knowing that we're going to face a tough enemy. In Psalm 18:17 David declares of the Lord: "He rescued me from my powerful enemies, from those who hated me and were *too strong for me*" (emphasis added).

Sometimes, the biggest barrier to freedom can be our own pride, masquerading as shame. If humility is "letting others know you for who you really are," as Bible teacher Joy Dawson said, then shame is the opposite, because we are just too ashamed to let others know us for who we really are, which often is rooted in pride.

Don't misunderstand me here: shame is a real issue, and it can be seriously debilitating, but we also need to recognize that if it is being fueled by the sin of pride, then nothing but confession and repentance is going to bring freedom from it. This can be a tough admission to make.

Researcher Brené Brown has spent many years studying shame and its effects. You might find it helpful to seek out videos of her speaking about it on YouTube. I'd also recommend reading one of her books on the subject, *Daring Greatly: How the Courage to Be*

Vulnerable Transforms the Way We Live, Love, Parent, and Lead. One of the tools she shares in it is to call out shame verbally when it appears, and to tell others about it so that we can be free from its lies.

I have adopted this practice and found it to be immensely helpful. When shame tries to raise its ugly, accusing face, I am able to look at it head-on and silence its accusing voice.

ACTION STEPS:

1. Pray and ask God to open your eyes to recognize when the voice of shame is speaking to you and begin to call it out.

2. Identify where your shame is coming from: is it from parents, teachers, old friends, or other family members?

3. As you face your shame, you may want to talk it through with a trained counselor.

#19 – Adopt Positive Affirmations

When Jesus was asked what the greatest commandment is, He gave a two-part answer. First, He said, we should love God with all our heart and with all our soul and with all our mind.

Then He went on: "This is the great and first commandment. And a second is like it: *You shall love your neighbor as yourself.* On these two commandments depend all the Law and the Prophets" (Matthew 22:35-40, emphasis added).

For years it has been a common practice in Christian circles to list and memorize, as much as possible, what the Scriptures say about who we are in Christ. It's very worthwhile, but for many of us it takes time to learn, and it can be difficult to really embrace these statements as our true identity. What can work faster is to write out self-affirmations of things that are true about us that can go really deep because they ring true about who we already know we are, and align with the Word of God.

I'm not saying that Scripture isn't powerful, of course. But merely reciting the words on the page of a Bible doesn't mean they have become real to us. For example, we know that we are children of God because "all who did receive him, who believed in his name, he gave the right to become children of God, who were born, not of blood nor of the will of the flesh nor of the will of man, but of God" (John 1:12-13). But if you really struggle with that concept, it can take a long time to believe it and its implications of family, love, and acceptance by God.

However, a number of years ago I had a revelation from Psalm 139:14: "I am fearfully and wonderfully made. Wonderful are your works..." I realized that meant if God took time and lots of consideration and thought into painstakingly making me, and that if He planned me from "before the foundation of the world" *(*Ephesians 1:4), then I must be really valuable! God doesn't ever make trash! He can't!

Therefore, I must be *really special*. So, the first affirmation that I ever wrote down that had real impact on me was a sort of personal paraphrase of what I knew God had said about me: "I am wonderful, because God doesn't make crap!" It had a deep impact on me when I would speak it out loud over myself, and suddenly I began to receive it deep within my heart.

ACTION STEPS:

To make sure that the affirmations that you begin to write down have some weight that will go down deep within your heart, here are a few guidelines as you compile your list:

1. Write down one affirmation for each year of your life, then add one after each birthday. Why so many? We need to counteract the many negative voices at work in our lives that can come from others, the enemy, and even ourselves.

2. Each affirmation should be something really true about you that is positive, and which goes deep into your soul when you speak it out—something meaningful that God has said about you and/or something deeply personal about yourself that is positive and true.

3. Pray and make sure that God is in agreement with what you are declaring over yourself. Be willing to make adjustments and corrections over time.

#20 – Face Your Loneliness

Loneliness is common to everyone. We're all going to experience it at some point in our lives. Maybe the saddest type of loneliness is when we are surrounded by a huge group of people and yet, because of a deep disconnection within, we can still feel totally alone.

When people work on identifying their "gates" (tool three), or when they discover what their triggers are (tool eight), it's very common for loneliness to be on the list. In the end, this is usually because we fear it and it creates "pain" for us. That may be because it's how we fear we are going to end up, or there is some kind of trauma from having been alone in the past. Whatever the reason, being on our own is just too painful because all of a sudden, we are alone with all of our issues and other "pains," which then leads to us acting out.

However, one of the oldest Christian spiritual disciplines is that of solitude, which is choosing to be alone, and withdrawing from people. How can something that so many of us view as painful and fearful be something positive that we should actually pursue rather than run from? I believe the answer is in our focus.

One of the most famous Christian authors to write about all this is Richard Foster (*Celebration of Discipline*), who says that "if we possess inward solitude we do not fear being alone, for we know that we are not alone." He goes on to say: "In solitude we are freed *from* our bondage to people and our inner compulsions, and we are freed *to* love God and know compassion for others."

So, when we are alone or find ourselves feeling lonely, we can "make lemons into lemonade" by actively embracing our situation and turning what might have been negative into a positive. We do this by changing our focus. Rather than dwell on what—or who—is absent, we take a moment to ground ourselves and focus on Jesus, "the author and perfecter of our faith" (Hebrews

12:2, ASV). He is the One who "has given us everything we need for life and godliness" (2 Peter 1:3, ISV), and who is "with us always, us to the very end of the age" (Matthew 28:20, NIV)—meaning we are never alone with Him, because He is always present.

Hebrews 13:5 (NIV) says that God has declared: "Never will I leave you; never will I forsake you." The Greek phrasing of this verse includes five negatives: you can't find a more emphatic truth about God's promise never to leave you alone than that. YOU ARE NEVER ALONE! It's impossible!

Finding strength in solitude isn't just a tool for dealing with compulsions and addictions—increasingly, it's an important practice to develop for all of life. That's because recent studies have found that, in our modern world, the person that you will spend most time with is not your parents, your spouse, your friends, or even your children, but yourself. We simply have to learn that we can be alone—with God—without being lonely.

ACTION STEPS:

1. Try it: Next time you are alone or feel lonely, turn to the Lord and decide that this feeling you are experiencing is, in fact, an opportunity and not a calamity!

2. Start by thanking Him for this time alone with Him. If you begin to feel pain for being alone, stay in it and invite God into it. Tell Him how you feel, really—be honest and descriptive.

3. It may take some time and a few tries for this to begin to work for you, but don't give up. This is an invaluable tool for all of your life, not just in dealing with compulsions or addictions.

...

If the regular-sized hammer isn't working by this stage, it may be time to call in the big guns. Go get the sledgehammer!

Remember, there is no shame in this. It does not mean things are hopeless; it simply is what it is. Indeed, as you pursue God in this, you are going to learn things about Him and discover a freedom that you've never known before!

SECTION THREE:
The Sledgehammer
(Late-Compulsion to Addiction)

#21 – Surrender Your Pride
Once I finally admitted that I had a sex addiction, the counselor I was seeing required me to start attending Sex Addicts Anonymous (SAA) meetings. To begin with, I went along thinking, "Oh, these guys just need Jesus! I should just preach the gospel to them and then all will be well." But then I realized how foolish I was being: I had no authority because I was in the same state of brokenness as them.

For the first six months, I was so ashamed that I would get into my truck after each meeting and let out a long, loud yell of anguish. I didn't realize it then, but that was evidence of my pride dying and my shame shrinking little by little each week.

In 2 Kings 5:1-14, there's the story of another man who had to surrender his pride to find healing. Naaman was a mighty man, the successful commander of the army of the Syrians who were among Israel's fiercest enemies at the time. But he had a secret sickness hidden beneath his armor, something that probably brought him great shame—and which he may have feared would have seen him ostracized if it became widely known. He had a really bad skin disease (possibly leprosy, though that's not absolutely clear).

Through a God-ordered series of events, an Israelite slave girl in his household told Naaman's wife that if he went to see the prophet Elisha, in Samaria, Elisha could heal him. Naaman decided to do this, but when he reached Elisha's house, the prophet didn't come to the door to greet his visitor. Instead, he sent a messenger with instructions for Naaman to go and bathe seven times in the Jordan.

Naaman was indignant. He "went away angry" (v.11), thinking that Elisha should have come out to greet someone as important as he was personally, and healed him there on the spot, in a powerful moment in front of everyone.

Does this sound familiar to you in any way? Can you relate? Have you perhaps thought God should act in a certain way? "I just need to have some man or woman of God pray for me. A dramatic encounter with the Lord will solve everything." Maybe you have gone forward for prayer at a service or in a ministry situation, but found your issue keeps coming back (something that happened to me over a period of years).

Like Naaman, I needed to be humbled. His pride was blocking his healing, and so was mine. Naaman had to come to the place of being willing to bathe in the river of his enemies, so to speak, and so did I. For me, that meant attending those SAA meetings, run by people that I looked down on (though I wasn't aware of it). My attitude was that they were nonbelievers while I was a Christian, so how could they possibly have answers that I needed? How could they know things I didn't?

But it wasn't really about knowledge—it was about pride. Deep in my heart, I thought I was better than non-Christians! I needed to come to the place of being willing to do whatever it took to get well, or I would never see healing.

The bottom line from Naaman's story and mine: Humble yourself! Do whatever it takes! Go wherever God is requiring you to go. It doesn't matter what people might think if they find out. Go wherever and do whatever it takes, and you will get free. Remember, "God opposes the proud but gives grace to the humble" (James 4:6).

Don't misunderstand me here. I'm not talking about doing something that is punishing you. This is not about being harsh for the sake of it—it's about hearing God's direction and following it. 1 Samuel 15:22 says that "to obey is better than sacrifice." It's in that spirit of resolution, rather than religiosity, that you need to be willing to do whatever God says to do. If that's attending a group that you don't want to go to, but you know God is saying, "Go," then go! If it means giving up your phone for a while, do it. If you have to change your job, do it.

Again, this isn't about being extreme to try to prove something to yourself or to God. But there is an old phrase used in recovery groups that says whatever you put in the way of your recovery you will end up losing, and I have to say, in my experience, this is true! "But I will look weird!" "What will others think of me?" "Why can't I just be 'normal'?" "Why do I have to have this issue?"

Look, we all have something in our lives that we have to deal with—this just happens to be yours. You may not be responsible for the root causes of your brokenness, the situation or circumstances that led to where you are now, but the hard truth is that it's now your responsibility to clean things up. And the good news is that if you want freedom in Christ, you can totally have it! You just have to be willing to do whatever it takes.

(And a short postscript here: Later in my SAA attendance, I did get to share the gospel with others there, many times. But I had to wait until I had gained the authority to speak, having experienced a significant measure of freedom, and could share from a place of humility, not pride.)

ACTION STEPS:

1. Pray and ask God for courage. Maybe start with the famous 12 Step prayer: "God, give me the serenity to accept the things I cannot change, the courage to change the things I can, and the wisdom to know the difference."

2. Share and process your feelings about this with your sponsor/coach. What does it mean for you to "bathe in the river of your enemies"? What do you have to change?

3. Ask God for the grace and courage (again) to do whatever He tells you that you need to do to get well. Then start doing it!

#22 – Practice Active Acceptance

If you want things to change, you have to start by accepting them the way they are now. That sounds almost contradictory, but it's not. I'm talking about giving up, not giving in. It's a kind of positive surrender that acknowledges the reality of whatever difficulty we may be facing without wishing it wasn't so, blaming someone else, or being resentful. Rather than just giving up, it means getting up and facing head-on whatever needs to be addressed.

But first you have to practice active acceptance. This isn't believing that God caused everything to happen in your life the way it has. He doesn't purpose evil, though He sometimes allows it for reasons that may never be fully clear to us this side of heaven. This is deep theological water—many books have been written about wrestling with the complexities of how a loving God permits bad things to happen.

Without minimizing those serious questions, I believe that, at the end of the day, we need to rest in God's sovereignty and focus on where and how we are responsible for the difficulties we face. This means that our issues are not someone else's fault. They are not because of our parents' wrong choices, or the abuse we suffered from the babysitter, or the exposure to porn from our cousins or friends growing up. These incidents might be contributing *reasons,* but we need to not blame them because that leaves us powerless.

Only when we recognize how events may have helped initiate our brokenness, but then go on to acknowledge how we ended up partnering with them—and that's why we're in this mess we are today—can we hope to find freedom. That may involve forgiving others for what they may have done and even letting go of some resentment toward God for not intervening as we believe He should have done.

Active acceptance is admitting that we have this problem, but we are not stuck with it or in it because God has got it and wants to set us free, if we work together with Him. This attitude of *acceptance* of our problem, but also *confidence* in God's ability to bring us into freedom is an essential tool to cultivate. It's why one of the readings that happens at almost every Sex Addicts Anonymous meeting declares:

> Acceptance is the answer to all my problems today. When I am disturbed, it is because I find some person, place, thing, or situation—some fact of my life—unacceptable to me, and I can find no serenity . . . Until I could accept my sex addiction, I could not stay abstinent; unless I accept life completely on life's terms, I cannot be happy. I need to concentrate not so much on what needs to be changed in the world as on what needs to be changed in me and in my attitudes.

ACTION STEPS:

1. Ask God to show you what is true and what is false in your belief system about His goodness. Ask Him to show you where you have exchanged the truth for denial.

2. Ask God to give you discernment and wisdom to know the difference between "having faith for healing," just "hoping it will go away," and taking some responsibility for working toward and cooperating in your own healing.

3. Talk these issues through with your sponsor or a counselor.

#23 – Treat Yourself Compassionately

If you are a follower of Jesus, then naturally you want to be like Him, right? Well, Psalm 145:8 (NIV) provides one of my favorite descriptions of what that looks like: "The LORD is gracious and compassionate, slow to anger and rich in love."

We all readily accept that we need to be like this toward others, but should we also treat ourselves the same way? My experience, personally and from having worked with many others seeking sexual wholeness, is that too often we think, "No!" Somehow, we have gotten this idea that we need to be hard on ourselves otherwise We'll get away with murder.

How sad! Because that simply is not consistent with God's character. He is "the same, yesterday and today, and forever" (Hebrews 13:8), and "The LORD is good to all; he has compassion on all he has made" (Psalm 145:9).

So, God is just and fair and loving and kind and compassionate *always*—within the Trinity in the Godhead *and* to all He has made. There are no exceptions; so that includes you and me. Therefore, I believe that we need to be the same.

Though it is counterintuitive for many of us, punishing oneself when you have messed up doesn't work. In the end, it only brings more shame—which then brings more pain, which then has to be dealt with, and which then often leads to more acting out. And on and on.

Please note that I am not condoning fuzzy psychobabble here. There has been increased awareness of the importance of mental health issues in recent times, and that's positive. But with that has come a lot of woolly thinking about "self-care" that doesn't really address our issues. Warm baths and candles and all that sort of stuff have their place, but they don't provide the ultimate answer to our needs, which is the loving truth of Jesus.

Note that I used "loving" and "truth" together. They can't be separated. So, what does loving ourselves look like? Being fair and firm, kind and consistent. Agape love has been described as wanting the highest good for the other person. If you had a seven-year-old child, would that mean letting them stay up all night eating ice cream, letting them view pornography, serving them vodka? Of course not. So why would you let yourself do those same things? Saying "no" in those circumstances is not being unkind, it is being truly loving.

If someone comes to you and confesses in humility and appropriate brokenness that they have acted out, would you yell at them and treat them harshly? No, you would treat them with compassion, love, and support. Then, lovingly, you should help them consider the appropriate consequences for what they have done and find appropriate solutions, so they won't act out again.

(There is only one occasion where you should speak strongly to someone or offer a rebuke in all this, and that is if they are in denial. For example, one person I met once told me that they had reduced their porn activity from five times a day to once a week. This was commendable progress, to be sure, but they now felt this reduced level of inappropriate behavior meant they were healthy enough to be involved in full-time ministry again. When I counseled this person that he needed more help to fully deal with his issues before he went into an even more stressful situation, potentially experiencing an even greater relapse, he balked, and decided that he was going ahead anyway. In such scenarios, having compassion means still speaking the truth in tough love.)

ACTION STEPS:

1. If you act out, or find yourself tempted, or in the "Middle" circle (tool 11), confess any sin but then extend grace to yourself. This will probably take some practice, but stop beating yourself up! Remember, "God's kindness is meant to lead you to repentance" (Romans 2:4). Learn to treat yourself the way that God treats you, with grace and mercy.

2. Work on expanding and enriching your "Outer" circle emphases—caring for your physical, mental, emotional, and spiritual health. That means eating well, exercising, getting enough sleep, and being around people who are emotionally healthy.

3. Ask others around to pray that you may grow in this area.

#24 – Complete the Steps

Once you are in a formal group focused on pursuing healing in this area, you need to fully pursue whatever program they offer. This will lead you to breakthrough, as long as you have joined a group with a proven track record of people having truly found long-term freedom.

I was fascinated to learn about the Christian roots of Alcoholics Anonymous (AA) and its 12 Step program, which many other groups have adopted and adapted. They can be traced back over 100 years to a visionary leader called Frank Buchman. As a young man in ministry for some time, he had a negative experience with his leaders and walked away with bitterness in his heart. But following a deep encounter with Jesus, he felt compelled to let go of his resentment and recognize that, in fact, he bore some responsibility for how he had reacted in the situation.

Buchman's experience led to him developing a discipleship program that was widely replicated, perhaps most notably in England, where what became known as the Oxford Group expanded across the world. Under its later name of Moral Re-Armament, this successful movement impacted whole spheres of society through its Christian principles.

Some members of the Oxford Group found that their six principles of discipleship—with many similarities to the Beatitudes of Matthew 5—were helpful in bringing freedom to many who struggled with alcoholism. And so AA was born in the 1930s, with the Oxford Group's six steps being developed into 12. Though the principles were later secularized to make them more accessible to a wider audience, the biblical principles they were based on remained the same.

Sex Addicts Anonymous (SAA), whose 12 Steps I base my groups on, was founded in 1977. I recommend attending SAA meetings and following all of these steps, while along the way reclaiming the biblical worldview that they were founded on. I have seen that, when followed in cooperation with the Holy Spirit, the 12 Steps can bring about some of the most incredible impact in a believer's life—even if they have no addictions whatsoever.

Here are the 12 Steps of SAA:

Step One: We admitted we were powerless over addictive sexual behavior—that our lives had become unmanageable.

Step Two: Came to believe that a Power greater than ourselves could restore us to sanity.

Step Three: Made a decision to turn our will and our lives over to the care of God as we understood God.

Step Four: Made a searching and fearless moral inventory of ourselves.

Step Five: Admitted to God, to ourselves and to another human being the exact nature of our wrongs.

Step Six: Were entirely ready to have God remove all these defects of character.

Step Seven: Humbly asked God to remove our shortcomings.

Step Eight: Made a list of all persons we had harmed and became willing to make amends to them all.

Step Nine: Made direct amends to such people wherever possible, except when to do so would injure them or others.

Step Ten: Continued to take personal inventory and when we were wrong promptly admitted it.

Step Eleven: Sought through prayer and meditation to improve our conscious contact with God as we understood God, praying only for knowledge of God's will for us and the power to carry that out.

Step Twelve: Having had a spiritual awakening as the result of these steps, we tried to carry this message to other sex addicts and to practice these principles in our lives.

This is a lot of work, but it is worth it! It's said that most people who attend these groups never get past Step 4, which is the backbone of healing and recovery. As we work through this step, we identify some of the major roots of our brokenness and the undealt-with fears and resentments that we unknowingly carry around with us.

Armed with this awareness, when you are triggered or tempted, there is now so little shame left related to them that you find yourself not as lured by the need to kill the pain anymore. The "need" to act out inappropriately has been significantly reduced because you have dealt with the pain in a correct and healthy way instead.

Some Christian teachers say, "You don't need 12 steps, you just need One step—and His name is Jesus!" And, yes, in many ways that's true, but only so far. It's a bit like saying we only need salvation, not discipleship. Jesus is always the only way to get truly free, but I followed Him for 34 years before I began to find true, deep, and lasting freedom in this area. I had inner healing deliverance from well-known ministry leaders, I followed programs of biblical meditation and memorization, and more besides—but only when I went after truly renewing my mind through following the 12 Steps did I find true transformation. There is no magic in them, but there is a pathway to freedom for those who follow them diligently.

How long is this process? If someone is truly diligent, they could probably complete the program in a year to 18 months. That may sound like a long time, but the reward—a lifetime of freedom—is more than worth it. And, in some ways, it's something you never complete, because the Steps are not so much a program as a way of life. It's like restoring an old car.

Once you have it running well, you just need to make sure it's well-maintained—keeping an eye on all the moving parts and doing any servicing that may be required, because road-wear (or life-wear) is inevitable.

ACTION STEPS:

1. Go online and find the nearest or easiest group for you to attend and go and try it!

2. Commit to attending for at least 10 weeks in a row and re-evaluate afterwards how you feel about it.

3. Process all of your feelings with your sponsor or others in the group.

#25 – Uncover the Roots

In his book *Unwanted: How Sexual Brokenness Reveals Our Way to Healing*, Jay Stringer talks about how finding the roots of our brokenness is so important. The reason is that, for many, a "road map" to our healing can be found right within our brokenness.

For example, I was sexually abused by my mother between the ages of 9 and 13, although I didn't fully recognize it as such until much later. My sexual acting out began when I was 12, but I couldn't figure out for the life of me why I would behave in such a manner. It was a mystery to me. Only when I finally began to pursue healing and recovery many years later and got help and counseling, did I start to realize that often for those involved in this type of behavior, it's not actually about sexual pleasure. Rather it is often primarily about attempting to try to get back the control they lost when they were abused or felt out of control.

Similarly, your "attraction template"—the type of people you find yourselves drawn to—or the type of porn that you may watch, or the things you may look at while acting out can all give key clues as to why you do what you do. What trauma happened, or what legitimate need was lacking that now you may have "sexualized"?

Traumatic experiences when we are young—which may or may not be sexual (from straight-up abuse in the form of unwanted physical contact, to mutual experimentation with other kids, or even first exposure to nudity by other people or unplanned circumstances)—can end up creating a kind of "first imprinting" on our brains.

There is a theory that when you get a song stuck in your head that you cannot get rid of, you should play it all the way through because that will help your brain relax. Otherwise, when that song is stuck in there your brain is trying to finish it for you.

In a much more complicated way, we need to identify and ask the question what was the "imprinting act" in regard to our sexuality that our brain is trying to "get rid of" so that it can bring about resolution and "complete the song in our head"? This will take time, and it may not be easy, but remember that God is on your side, and He wants to help you in this. He wants your freedom—more than you do—because He loves you so much.

For me, it was about 18 months before I finally understood my deepest root insecurity. After being in counseling, going to SAA meetings, seeing my sponsor weekly, and working my way through the 12 Steps, as well as reading the books I have mentioned, I finally understood the core root issue for me from which everything else followed was that I didn't feel like a man, or I wasn't somehow "man enough."

Once I realized this, I was able to change my belief and look at the real truth of what God said, and all of the other evidence, and begin to believe the truth about my manhood.

Today I am able to share that freely because it no longer is a question for me. That unwholesome root, based on a lie, has been dug out and in its place is a healthy awareness of who I am, as someone anchored in God's love and acceptance. I have a confidence that I am man enough in Him and that bears fruit in my life and the lives of others.

Action Steps:

1. Begin to journal what you think you are attracted to sexually and why. Ask the Holy Spirit to begin to show you the roots of those attractions. Ask Him to begin to lead you to the main root underneath them all. Be patient; it may take some time to get to this point.

2. Process all this with your counselor and/or sponsor. Explore with them where you think the root incidents of possible trauma or imprinting occurred. Again, invite the Holy Spirit into those memories and see what He has to say about them.

3. Consider seeking help from experienced ministers. While I believe that we can be too quick to claim that "the devil made me do it," there certainly can be a demonic element to why these roots can be difficult to dig out.

#26 – Get a Counselor

Many years ago, I thought that counseling was something only for the "really bad cases." Thankfully, I have matured in my thinking, and I have actually been helped many times by some very gifted counselors.

An experienced therapist can be God's provision to help us when we cannot help ourselves. In partnership with the group that you are a part of, and your sponsor, they can help you understand your trauma and many of the roots of your brokenness.

Now, there are definitely good counselors and bad ones, or at least ones who are a better fit for you. So here are some things to consider as you seek a therapist who can help you. Get referrals from friends. If they have been helped, there is a good chance that the same counselor may be a good fit for you (though not necessarily).

- Do this therapist's values align with yours? Do they have the same approach to life that you do? Do they follow Jesus? Do they understand your perception of your calling? Do they have a biblical worldview?

- Do you feel at ease when you are with them? Do you feel comfortable sharing anything and everything with them? Do you feel like you can trust them? Do you feel safe?

- Do you feel like they are giving you good advice or helping you discover more about yourself that is true that you didn't know already?

It may take some time to answer these questions. For example, on one occasion I remember not feeling anything during my session with a counselor, nor did I come away with any major revelations from our time together.

But then, throughout that following week, things happened or came up that made sense in ways that hadn't in the past. After maybe three to six appointments with someone you will probably know if they are a good fit for you.

At some point, it might be helpful to stop seeing a counselor for a season, to give you time to reflect on all that you have worked on together so far, but don't stop going just because you feel uncomfortable to a degree—that could mean they are getting too close to the truth of what your problem is, or you're moving in denial.

Seeing a counselor requires bravery and humility, which means being able to face up to the shame that we all carry to varying degrees in our lives. Finally, you may want to consider permitting your sponsor/coach to be in touch with your therapist so that they can compare notes. Bringing their understanding and insights together can hopefully speed up your process of healing.

Action Steps:

1. Ask family and trusted friends if they know any good counselors that you might reach out to.

2. Check them out online and see if they are available to meet for an exploratory first meeting. At the end of it, see what they would recommend, and evaluate how they answered your questions above.

3. If you feel like there is a good fit on both sides, continue with what they recommend.

#27 – Assess Your Accountability

Ensuring that you have the right person as one of your primary accountability partners makes a huge difference, but it's not as cut-and-dried as it might seem at first glance. Most people automatically think about someone very close to them—their husband or wife, their boyfriend or girlfriend, or their best friend. That goes without saying, right? Well, not necessarily.

Now, it is generally true that your spouse should know everything about you, particularly in the area of your sexual involvement. 1 Corinthians 7:4 teaches: "For the wife does not have authority over her own body, but the husband does.

Likewise the husband does not have authority over his own body, but the wife does." In other words, we are not allowed to do anything with our bodies in a sexual way once we are married without our spouse's consent, because we simply do not have the authority to do that.

The word *authority* here is pretty strong. It's the same one used in Mark 3:15 when we read that Jesus gave His disciples authority to cast out demons. Let's be clear: this instruction to the Corinthian church does not give you the right to "command" your spouse in Jesus's name to do certain things, but it does mean that we need to have the fear of the Lord about what we do with our bodies sexually because it will have repercussions on our precious life partner.

Having said that, don't just assume that your spouse automatically has to become your main accountability partner regarding the details of your sexual brokenness. Yes, they should know for sure if you have been unfaithful to them, but for some spouses, it is just too much for them to know all the details.

Then there is the dynamic that can arise where spousal accountability moves into an unhealthy controlling situation, where the sober partner gets so involved that they try to manage their spouse's behavior to stop themselves from getting hurt. So, if you are married, you need to clearly communicate boundaries and expectations of what should be shared between both partners.

It might be helpful to get some outside input from a counselor or sponsor to determine what is best for you both. (Additionally, a spouse whose husband or wife is dealing with sexual brokenness could benefit immensely from seeing a counselor themselves, to help them process all their thoughts and feelings about the situation.)

The one who is struggling should share everything with their sponsor and then determine how much their spouse should be involved in the practical specifics of their healing.

This same question may need to be addressed regarding your closest friends or other family members. Should they be involved in detail?

If so, how much? Who are the ones who need to know everything, and will truly hold you accountable, and who are those who are meant to know in more general terms and who are best suited to being your prayer and moral support through this healing process?

If you are not clear on this, all kinds of challenging things can happen that will potentially affect what have been close relationships.

If this is not handled with wisdom, it may only cause more stress, which can in turn lead to more temptation, and then to more acting out to kill the pain of the situation.

Action Steps:

1. Assess how involved your spouse, family member(s), or close friend(s) currently are in your recovery process? Does this need to change in any way? Why?

2. Will it be best for both them and you to have them more or less involved in holding you accountable?

3. Talk this through your counselor and/or sponsor and pray for God's wisdom and leading.

#28 – Don't Act In

One of the dangers of unwise efforts to avoid acting out is that we can end up "acting in" instead. If acting out is a chaotic response to our brokenness and unhealthy emotions, then acting in is a rigid, almost religious response. It's not uncommon for those in an addictive level of brokenness to swing between these two extremes.

After following their addiction into new areas or levels of degree, they will then try to counter by embracing extreme forms of discipline and self-denial. For a time, it may look like real repentance and growth, but after a while it will swing back the other way again, and so on.

Before I found and began to use the tools in this book, I fit this pattern pretty well. As I mentioned earlier, I didn't act out for more than three years after meeting the woman who would become my wife. Looking back, I can now see that was because in courting and marrying the girl of my dreams, for the first time I began to experience the most real intimacy I had ever known to that point in my life.

Unfortunately, that only dealt with the symptoms, masking the root problem issues deep inside. (This is why I ask those who join my group not to date anyone until they have at least six months 'sobriety so that they know they are beginning to find true freedom and not just masking their issue through a romantic relationship.)

In Alcoholics Anonymous they call this being a "dry drunk," where you may have stopped drinking but you're still an alcoholic on the inside, in your mind. If this is the case, it will just be a matter of time, as with me, before you will most likely swing back again to acting out.

I would go through times of exercising what I thought was—and which outwardly seemed to be—great discipline. But it was motivated by the wrong attitude. It was really more a form of self-punishment than self-care. There is a difference between on the one hand being tempted to act out and remaining at peace, knowing who we are in Christ, and relying on His grace and strength, and on the other resisting temptation in our own strength, white-knuckling it with all of our might.

If we resist in this second way, we can become so uptight that we can end up being stressed out and rude to everyone around us. Because of this, we have then created a new type of "pain" which will then lead us to want to act out to kill this new pain. It's simply an unsustainable lifestyle. But if we use the tools in this book, and others that we find, that bring true, deep, mind-renewed healing, we will find ourselves being able to resist from the right motives and attitudes—not acting in, but saying no to temptation from a place of peace.

There are two ditches on this road to recovery. Acting out tends to be excessive and done sometimes out of anger or self-hatred, often in a defiant, not-thinking-about-the-consequences way.

Acting in tends to deprive itself unnecessarily and to a damaging degree, often out of fear of acting out. Rather than go to either extreme, we have to make sure that we stay centered on Jesus and His path to freedom.

ACTION STEPS:

1. Reflect on where you feel disciplined or feel very strongly about a certain behavior. Is this a conviction from a place of peace and rest or does it come from a pressure you feel to "master" this thing because otherwise you will be unacceptable? If so, this may not be a healthy practice, but acting in.

2. Talk about this and process it with your counselor and/or sponsor.

3. Pray for God's wisdom and insight.

#29 – Share with Wisdom

Starting out on this path to healing, many find it really difficult to share where they are at. This often is because of shock and denial at first: we just can't believe that we are "that bad." Then, once we begin to deal with shame and we begin to trust the community of people that God has led us to, those that have struggled or still do in the same ways as we do, we begin to get more comfortable telling our story.

Taking the first of the 12 Steps, we share our whole brokenness history in detail with our sponsor and they don't respond badly; in fact, we find it feels good to be finally free and share absolutely every detail with someone else, maybe for the first time.

Then, as we grow further, and others around us share in our group, we can become more relaxed and realize it is an advantage to share more because we grow in freedom that way. It's at this point, however, that we can make a mistake. We can begin sharing in the wrong places and in the wrong ways, with the wrong people.

How can this be? "I thought that you said that humility was the key to freedom?" Well, yes, it is, but that does not mean you have to start telling everyone everything inappropriately. We need to be careful with whom we share our brokenness and process it, particularly the details.

Before you do, consider that many people may not understand (even if you think they will) and may treat you differently in a way that is unhelpful for your recovery.

We also need to take others 'needs into consideration. This is not just about you. Sometimes our need to share can be inappropriate and even damaging to others if they are not mature enough or simply not ready to hear things that maybe they have never even thought of before. In fact, sharing unwisely and carelessly can even be considered a form of sexual abuse towards others as we cross appropriate boundaries. Not everyone wants or needs to know your whole story.

So please be cautious, but not fearful. Walk in tension somewhere between these scriptures:

> But sexual immorality and all impurity or covetousness must not even be named among you, as is proper among saints . . . For it is shameful even to speak of the things that they do in secret. – Ephesians 5:3, 12

and:

> Therefore, confess your sins to one another and pray for one another, that you may be healed. The prayer of a righteous person has great power as it is working. – James 5:16

We need to check our motives. Are we sharing because we want to be humble and transparent, or perhaps because we want to help and encourage others by talking about how God has brought us into freedom?

Again, the key is humility—it's possible to share our story for the wrong reasons, like trying to impress people or have them feel sorry for us. We are looking for the sort of healthy tension that we read in Ephesians 4:29:

> Let no corrupting talk come out of your mouths, but only such as is good for building

up, as fits the occasion, that it may give grace to those who hear.

Seek to be led by the Holy Spirit and ask your sponsor or coach for wisdom in these things and you will not go far wrong.

ACTION STEPS:

1. Ask God to show you who you should share your issues with outside of those that you need to.

2. Review this over time, and if you do share with people, make sure that it is done in a sensitive way, particularly where you are taking responsibility for your issues and not blaming others.

#30 – Face the Fear

Once we have identified the roots and triggers of our sexual brokenness, we can begin to develop habits and practices that bring us into greater freedom. That's what this book is all about. But it's not to say that we will never face temptation again; we just know how to deal with it should it arise. We need to remain vigilant, which all the tools in this book encourage.

Though we are never completely "out of the woods" when it comes to temptation, for some people the biggest threat to their long-term recovery is not the actual triggers that used to derail them. It's the fear of losing their sobriety. I remember when I'd experienced two years of good health and recovery. I was grateful for where I was, but I found myself thinking, "Two years is great, but I'll never make it to four—or seven, or ten." My fear of what might happen was actually endangering me, because it was a "pain" I wanted to suppress or avoid, just as I had done previously in my life.

One time, in a group meeting, I expressed this fear of not being able to keep my sobriety for the long haul, for all of the years ahead. The other guys chuckled and then reminded me of one of the main tenets of the program: it's all about "one day at a time."

As you are reading this, what time of the day is it? How many more hours are left in your day that you need to remain sober before you fall asleep tonight? Do you think that, by using the tools in this book, you can stay sober until then? If yes, then that's all you have to worry about! Remember, Jesus said, "Do not be anxious about tomorrow, for tomorrow will be anxious for itself. Sufficient for the day is its own trouble" (Matthew 6:34). We are not promised tomorrow! But should you wake up tomorrow, do you think that you'll be able to stay sober until you go back to bed again? In this way, days become weeks, weeks become months, and months become years. You can only ever gain and maintain sobriety one day at a time.

I came to realize that if I am afraid that I am going to lose my sobriety, then I probably am going to do so, because it's like a self-fulfilling prophecy. So, I have learned not to give room to fear of the future—the what-ifs. Rather, I focus on where I have come from and where I am today, knowing that with God's grace and using the tools I have collected, I can continue to walk in freedom.

As I have said, I don't believe the devil is behind all our troubles, but he definitely tries to exploit them. That voice telling you that you can't keep your freedom isn't from God, it's from the one the Bible calls the father of lies (John 8:44, NIV) and "the accuser of our brothers" (Revelation 12:10). Don't listen to him!

Action Steps:

1. Break it down. Can you guarantee you are going to remain sober for the next however many years? No, but you can take it, as AA says, "one day at a time." When you find yourself being fearful, remind yourself that, with the truths and tools you have discovered, you can remain sober for the rest of this day. And tomorrow you can do the same thing again.

2. When you find yourself facing fear, reach out to your support network in the same way you would if you were facing temptation.

3. Use the affirmations you have developed to counter the lies you are hearing with the truths you know.

Afterword

So, there you have it—all the tools you'll ever need to achieve 100 percent freedom from sexual brokenness. If only! In all honesty, I cannot make that promise to you.

However, I can say from my increasing age and experience of seeing more and more people achieving lasting breakthroughs using these tools that if you really do apply and use the ones that help you, and if you continue to pursue them for the rest of your life, then you *will* get free.

Many people ask me, "Well, how long will it take?" We all want everything instantly, or as fast as possible, right?

I understand that desire, but it doesn't quite work like that. Remember, this is all about *progress, not perfection*. In fact, our desire to "be perfect" is often a sign of our ongoing brokenness, while to desire to be healthy the way that Jesus wants us to be healthy is a beautiful thing.

One of my previous counselors, Steve, used to say that if it takes you about two hours to walk into a cave, then it usually takes you about two hours to walk out of it!

Will your journey always seem to be as all-encompassing and demanding as it does in the early days and even months? No. It's a bit like learning to drive a car. When you first get behind the wheel, you are (rightly) hyper-alert about all that you are doing.

But as you get more experienced, some of those things that you have to concentrate on to begin with become second nature. Instead of reminding yourself to check in the rearview mirror every time before you change lanes, you just do it automatically.

Then, one day, you find yourself pulling into your driveway and you wonder, "How did I get here?" The process of driving is so much a part of your muscle memory that you just do it.

It's sort of the same with recovery from sexual brokenness. I still have days when I face temptation and have to consciously use some of the tools I have identified to help me. But, for the most part, they are just such a part of my life that I use them without even being aware of doing so.

Is there a price to be paid for freedom? Yes, but it is so worth it. I've been completing this manuscript as athletes have gathered from around the world for the latest Olympic Games. It has been inspiring to see the dedication they have given over many years in pursuit of a gold medal.

But how much more rewarding could it be for you to find true freedom and the abundant life Jesus promised?

- To draw a line in the sand with this generation and say, "No more" to all the sexual brokenness that came through previous generations and that has been passed down to you through your family?
- To not have to bring that baggage into your marriage or pass it on to your children and their future generations?
- To be that man or that woman that says, "It ends here, with me!"

Wouldn't that be worth it?
Yes, it would.
With all the tools I have shared now in your hands, the decision is yours. And I'm cheering you on.

TRIGGERS

- Emotions (**B L A H S T O**)
  - **B** ored
  - **L** onely
  - **A** ngry
  - **H** ungry
  - **S** tressed
  - **T** ired
  - **O** verwhelmed
- Fight with partner
- Particular music/song
- Specific person
- Memory
- Criticism
- Smells
- Movie/TV show
- Location/place
- Disappointment
- Money anxiety

RITUALIZATION EXAMPLES

- Clothing/apparel
- Grooming
- Perfume/cologne
- Texting
- Personal/intimate conversation
- Eye contact/smiling
- Fantasizing
- Flirting/innuendos
- Touching
- Driving to specific locations
- Drinking
- Social media
- Movies
- Looking for arousing content
- Finding a private location
- Certain body positions

CYCLE OF ADDICTION

1. **WOUNDS → BELIEFS → SHAME**
2. **TRIGGER**
3. **OBSESSION/FANTASY**
4. **RITUALIZATION**
5. **COMPULSION/ACTING OUT BEHAVIOR**
6. **DESPAIR**
7. **GUILT & SHAME**
8. **RESOLVE + VOWS**

WOUNDS

- Childhood attachment injuries
- Emotional, physical, sexual abuse, and neglect

BELIEFS

- I am a bad, unworthy person (shame).
- No one would love me as I am.
- No one will meet my needs/nurture me.
- Sex (or an intense relationship) is my most important need/way I feel loved.

"God isn't good enough, doesn't love me enough, won't or isn't powerful enough to meet my needs."

CYCLE OF ADDICTION DIAGRAM
Developed by:
Patrick Carnes, Ph.D.
Originally edited by:
Marnie Frree, MA, LMFT, CSAT;
Laura M. Brotherson, MS, MFT (2013).
Adapted and edited by Richard Thompson (2024).

Understanding the Cycle of Addiction

In 12 Step literature, addiction is described as "cunning, baffling, and powerful," and that is so true. Sometimes, just when you think you have everything under control, it can rear its head again. This diagram may help you recognize and understand the type of cycle that commonly occurs in any kind of addiction, though we are focusing on sexual addiction and compulsive behaviors.

1. As you can see, everything stems from the wounds that we carry. These can usually be traced back to our childhood, or may happen later in life, and would include, but not be limited to, attachment and abuse issues. Sadly, these experiences shape our belief systems about all of life, even if many of them are rooted in lies or misperceptions of reality. It is really important to become aware of these core beliefs, as they will always end up determining our actions. Many of us carry all kinds of beliefs that we are unaware of that lead to unconscious behaviors that can damage ourselves or others. Shame, sometimes deeply held and felt, is also developed from these beliefs.

2. As we go through our everyday lives, we experience normal incidents that can become

"triggers," or reminders of past hurt, abuse, or shame. As a result, some level of "pain" occurs within us which we then feel we have to deal with, often unconsciously. Sometimes we can develop healthy patterns to deal with these occurrences, such as reaching out to God and to others for help to process them. However, many times, we learn to numb the pain by acting out inappropriately (and, if you are reading this book, that's most probably in unhealthy sexual behaviors).

3. First comes fantasy or obsession and unhealthy thinking. Sometimes these can be manifested through intrusive sexual thoughts, which are often a sign of undealt-with trauma or past hurts.

4. As this type of thinking continues, either consciously or otherwise, we can find ourselves preparing for what's ahead through ritualization. This is when we begin to place ourselves in what we think will be the best and most satisfying situation for our upcoming acting out. The amount of time that it can take from the point of experiencing a trigger that leads into obsessive thinking and ritualization to the point of acting out can vary greatly—anywhere between seconds and even months.

5. Finally, you reach the point of acting out in whatever form it takes for you. The sense of satisfaction or euphoria from this numbing of the

pain is very brief, relative to what came before and what comes afterward.

6. Almost immediately, any sense of relief or comfort is overtaken by one of despair which, if you are a believer, we would probably call conviction from the Holy Spirit.

7. At this point, we may experience an interesting cycle within the larger cycle that may involve a combination of emotions and thoughts. Most likely, you will feel guilt and shame, which only increases your pain. This can then lead to you needing to act out again to kill that pain, leading you deeper and deeper into the cycle.

8. This process may be accompanied by your making a resolve or a vow to "never do this again!" And, in that moment, you are able to mean it—but, sadly, that is all it is: a moment. Very soon, the pain of the guilt and shame strangely subside until the cycle begins again. There's a new trigger, which leads to obsession and fantasy, and so the cycle begins all over again!

If you would like more help or resources, you can use your camera to scan the QR code on this page, which will link you to an email address where you can request online personal coaching, additional resources, or you can simply ask questions. God bless you!

Assessing Your Situation

You have probably picked this book up because you're concerned about your sexual brokenness to at least some degree. So, I'd suggest that reading it all the way through could be surely helpful.

However, it will probably be advantageous for you to have a sense of how significant an issue you are dealing with. This simple self-assessment may help. Of course, it's not detailed and definitive, but it can provide some measure of understanding of where you are.

Answer yes or no to the following 12 questions fairly quickly; don't overthink your response.

1. Do you find yourself obsessively thinking about sexual fantasies or behaviors? Are you often preoccupied or distracted by such thoughts?

2. Have you attempted to stop some sexual behaviors but been unsuccessful, even though you may have tried many times? Have you begun to feel like this has more control of you than you do of it?

3. Do your sexual fantasies or behaviors conflict with the standards of your personal faith or belief system, or your community?

4. After sexual behavior, with yourself or others, have you felt regret for behaving in a way

different to what you would normally prefer or choose?

5. Do you have any past experiences of trauma, abuse, or neglect (sexual or otherwise)?

6. Have you found yourself being willing to disengage with those closest to you, or those that you love most, to engage in sexual behavior?

7. Have you ever lost a job, been willing to break the law, or engaged in sexual behavior without thought of consequences (such as pregnancy or disease?

8. Has your sexual behavior affected your relationships negatively, causing you to avoid emotional intimacy with others?

9. Do you lead a double life? Or have you ever lied to anyone about your sexual behavior or kept secrets about it from those closest to you?

10. Have you hurt others by your sexual behavior, either physically, mentally, or emotionally? Has anyone important to you ever shown concern about any of your sexual behavior?

11. Has there been an escalation over time in your sexual behavior, either its frequency or its extreme activity, to get excitement, or to deal with difficult things or boredom?

12. Have you ever sought help from others with this problem before?

That may have been uncomfortable for you, but thanks for answering honestly! Here's where you probably stand:

One or Two "Yeses": There is some kind of issue there, but it's early days. Taking a closer look at your life with some of the tools in this book could help you establish boundaries that prevent things from escalating. Remember, what is unaddressed remains unhealed.

Three to Six "Yeses": Some unhealthy ways of dealing with past pain have started to sink roots into your life. There is a level of compulsion to some of the things you do. But take heart, you can face them and weed them out and find a freedom you never thought possible.

Seven or more "Yeses": You've confirmed what you probably already knew, deep in your heart of hearts: sexual brokenness controls your life to an increasing degree. But there is good news—admitting this is the case is the first step to freedom! Using the tools in this book can help you keep walking in that direction.

As I said, this is only a simple assessment exercise meant to stimulate you to action. There are others you can find online. Don't dwell too much on the results but let them be a challenge to change and an invitation to growth.

About the Author

Richard Thompson has been serving with Youth With A Mission (YWAM) since 1986. His work has taken him to some 60 countries around the world so far, and he is looking forward to adding more to that list because he loves being part of the Great Commission calling.

Born and raised in Liverpool, England, Richard earned a degree in geology from Sheffield University and worked in people and technical management as a chocolate technologist for Nabisco UK before following God's call into ministry.

He completed his initial ministry training in the U.K. in 1986. From then until 1996, he served and ended up leading the YWAM ministry of GO-Teams based in Amsterdam, the Netherlands, sharing the gospel in evangelistic outreaches across West and Eastern Europe and in the United States.

From 1996 to 2012, Richard pioneered and led the YWAM ministry center established in Las Vegas, Nevada, with an emphasis on "Serving the Church, Changing the City and Reaching the Nations." From 2012 to 2018, while remaining in Las Vegas, and still a part of YWAM, he also served as the pastor of ministry development for Grace City Church.

Since 2018, Richard has been part of the staff of the University of the Nations, YWAM Kona Campus, in Kona, Hawaii, which is currently the largest missionary training center in the world. He serves there as a part of the Fire & Fragrance ministry and leads the BE FREE ministry he founded in 2019. He also travels internationally to expand this ministry to help anyone in YWAM (or anyone else!) find freedom from sexual brokenness, and to speak on missions and Christian discipleship.

Richard has four children that he is very proud of: three on earth and one in heaven.

You can contact him at:

Befree4ever777@gmail.com

Made in the USA
Middletown, DE
21 February 2025

71537572R00059